WHY YOU MUST LEAD

FRESH PERSPECTIVE FOR EXTRAORDINARY LEADERSHIP

ERNEST ADEMOLA EHIGIE

The Accolades says it all

This book – Why you must lead- talks about the very core of leadership and its essence. Ernest did not only dwell on the nitty-gritty of leadership but how leadership brings about innovation in various aspects of our existence. I recommend this book to everyone at the top and aspiring leaders especially our young people. Well done Ernest!

Yomi Badejo-Okusanya
GMD, CMC Connect (Perception Managers) and President, African Public Relations Association (APRA).

''Great leaders at various times have shaped history differently. Ademola in this masterpiece reflects leadership with depth of within, with understanding and with the intent of giving value as well as a calling . This is meant to shapen the reader's disposition in exhibiting a positive character for a truly successful leadership experience''

Prince Adeyemi Adebayo.
E-Revenue Gateway Ltd

"What a great honor to be associated with Ernest. I have known him back in the days in the university as a student leader. Ernest had since known his "WHY" both for leadership and life in general. It is no surprise to handle this great book full of leadership nuggets for living a purpose-driven life. The stories therein are timely and relevant for everyone. I do not hesitate to recommend this book to all who care to understand "the Why" in leadership."

David Asanga
Inspirational Speaker and Social Reformer
Kampala, Uganda

Let me appreciate the good work you did on this job. It was insightful, precise and soul searching. Indeed, I have been blessed by reading it. This book will make an impact and I am excited at the prospect of it, and I have to thank God that you stood up to be counted as one that has the potential to lead. More power to your elbow and may this be the start of many more.

Tobi Adeosun
Oil and Gas Consultant.

This book is a great reminder of the reason for our existence; to lead, to influence, to impact. Using the real life experiences of everyday people who simply stepped forward when it mattered most, it beautifully illustrates the fact that leadership is not a position or title. Leadership is simply stepping out of the crowd or stepping up to take the lead.

Lola Olusola
Serial Entrepreneur, Co-Founder Horizon Shores Nig. Ltd.

This book (Why You Must Lead) is an applaudable contribution to the subject of leadership. Ernest interestingly posits that leadership is a primary need of mankind, which every human has innate capacity to undertake effectively, at every phase of life, once they have answered the grand question - WHY? He also states that worthwhile leadership should be undertaken for GOD, Self and Humanity. Ernest's practical view and passion for the subject is evident on the pages of the book, as he uses everyday examples/ experiences of people (including himself) to drive home his point, which makes the book a good read.

Ige Adelayo Esq.
Partner, F&C Legal Practitioners

WHY YOU MUST LEAD
FRESH PERSPECTIVE FOR EXTRAORDINARY LEADERSHIP

Amazon

Kindle Direct Publishing (KDP)

Created by
5 Syllables

Why You Must Lead

Copyright © 2018 by Ernest Ademola Ehigie

All rights reserved.

No part of this publication may be reproduced, stored in or introduced into a retrieval system, or transmitted, in any form or by any means (electronic, mechanical, photocopying, recording or otherwise), without the prior written permission of both the copyright owner and the above publisher of this book. The scanning, uploading, and distribution of this book via the Internet or via any other means without the permission of the publisher is illegal and punishable by law.

Please purchase only authorized electronic editions and do not participate in or encourage electronic piracy of copyrightable materials. Your support of the author's rights is appreciated. While the author has made every possible effort to ensure that the information contained in this book is accurate at the time of going to press. The author and publisher cannot accept responsibility for any errors or omissions, however caused. No responsibility for loss or damage occasioned to any person acting, or refraining from action, as a result of the material in this publication can be accepted by the author, editors, or the publisher.

Written permission must be secured from the author and/or publisher to use or reproduce any part of this book, except for brief quotations in critical reviews or articles.

Unless otherwise indicated, all Scripture quotations are from The Message Bible Version of the Holy Bible.

Cover design director, design and book format:
Joshua Nkemjika Ekeh
Vixxel Branding

Copyright © 2018 Ernest Ademola Ehigie

Amazon: Amazon.com/author/contentking
LinkedIn: https://www.linkedin.com/in/ehigieernest/
Twitter: @IAmContentKing
Instagram: @iamcontentking
Email: officialcontentking@gmail.com

LEADERSHIP

It is the only way you were born to live. The only way to true fulfillment in life.

Your true identity is embedded in living the life of service.

Your ultimate purpose in life lies in stepping into leadership.

Being a leader makes you an authentic person.

It is setting yourself up for a life of maximizing your full potentials.

Knowing that leadership is mandatory, walking in the path where your gift, talent, passion, unique experience, interest, skill and calling becomes the best decision.

Leadership is not a secondary endeavour, it is our primary check list;

For God

For You

For Humanity.

DEDICATION

It is with great honour that I dedicate this book to the memory of **Dr. Ameyo Stella Adadevoh**. Whose story as I visited in the cause of writing this book, led to the discovery of new perspective on her heroic act of sacrifice that saved a nation of over 170 million people, the most populous African nation, and the world from becoming a ghost land overnight.

ACKNOWLEDGEMENT

This work is a typical narrative of the African communal living where everyone comes together to ensure the success of one, because the success of one impacts on the success of everyone.

This communal lifestyle came with immense value, and hopefully is evolving into collaboration and co-working business environment of today. Modernity is nothing without the connection that humanity brings.

This part of this book is perhaps one of my favourite as I have the opportunity to showcase the irreplaceable place of being surrounded by great people. And I have no problem if this part spill over many pages of this book because the people mentioned here are definitely worth it.

But first, my unreserved accolades and high praise goes to God, the giver of life and content that makes us unique and special. He is the one that gives me the power to will and to do according to His good pleasure. Thank You Lord.

To my parents, I love and appreciate you Pa John and Rose Ehigie. Thank you for your unreserved believe in me. You are special! Thank you Sir and Ma. Thank you.

To my siblings Bola, Timothy, Bright and Kayode Ehigie, thank you for all that you are to me, and all that you do for me. Your place in my story is inestimable. Thank you.

To Brian Tracy, your class on book publishing was the force that struck the 'can do' spirit which birthed this great piece. Thank you.

To Dr. Sam Adeyemi for your legendary exemplary leadership that inspires me to be a better leader everyday. Thank you.

To my mentor, Kola Oyeneyin and your wife Eyitope; to be so interested in this raw material of a person is amazing. Your concern and support to see me grow is highly commendable. Thank you Sir and Ma. Thank you.

To Joshua Nkemjika Ekeh for this book design, cover page and the entire formatting. The speed at which you deliver this excellent work is amazing! And most importantly your body language to the success of this project inspires me. Thank you my friend and brother. Thank you.

To Oluwatobi Adeosun, Adedamola Jaiyeoba and Oreoluwa

Sotade my quintessential editors/editorial advisory board, you are the real deal. You are such a great support. How you disrupt your busy schedule to proofread this book is commendable. Thank you.

To Lola Olusola, from the very first day I shared this idea with you, the project took a new life. And for allowing me to share your rare leadership story in this book. Thank you for the Grace and direction you brought into this project. Thank you Ma. Thank you.

To Barrister Ige Adelayo, Pastor Grace Ofili, and David Asanga; for sharing your leadership stories, and your embrace of this idea even when it was yet raw. As well as your support and encouragement paid off greatly. Thank you.

To the US Consulate in Lagos Nigeria, Samuel A. Eyitayo the librarian at the US Consulate when this book was published, and Arthur Zulu; for facilitating the free class on Kindle Publishing organised by the Consulate, I am forever grateful. The class was a major turning point for the success of this book. Thank you.

To Sam O. Salau, Abbey Dollar Ashade, Ilesanmi Idowu

(McMofe), Fehintola Lawal-Are, Rotimi Olushola; your great and unique support, counsel, intervention and timely guide contributed immensely to the success of this master piece. Thank you.

To my Adullam Network tribe, I say may the force be with you. Thank you for inspiring me daily. Thank you.

To all the shining stars I shared their stories in this book, to those who contributed one way or the other to the success of this book, whose name were not mentioned here, I appreciate you beyond words can express. You are all special! Thank you.

Ernest ADEMOLA ABIDOYE Ehigie

TABLE OF CONTENT

	Dedication	*viii*
	Acknowledgement	*ix*
	Table of Content	*xiii*
CHAPTER ONE	*Why Leadership - The Essence*	*14*
CHAPTER TWO	*Know Your 'Why'*	*31*
CHAPTER THREE	*Lead for God*	*61*
CHAPTER FOUR	*Lead for You*	*83*
CHAPTER FIVE	*Lead for Humanity*	*118*
	References	*169*

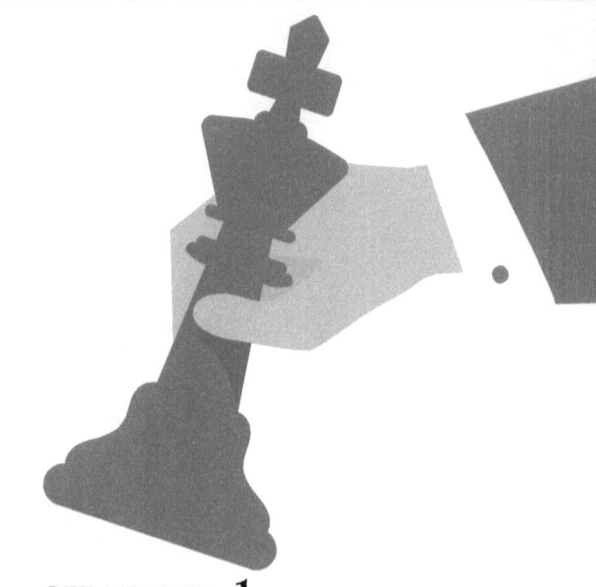

CHAPTER 1

INTRODUCTION

WHY LEADERSHIP - THE ESSENCE

WHAT YOU HAVE ALWAYS BELIEVED ABOUT leadership may be on the verge of a major paradigm shift. A new frontier of leadership mindset is staring at you in form of a book. If you are not sure of your capacity to fully, and wholly embrace the unconventional thoughts in this stroke of genius, you might as well take this in piecemeal for better self-profiting. But one thing is for sure, no information no matter how small, leaves you the same way once exposed to it. Same way you do not remain the same when you embark on a journey. And this is a novel leadership perspective, and promises to be a mind shifting journey into the business of leadership.

You are about to delve into the world of some radical

findings, and unpopular discovery that will change your leadership perspective forever. This book is going to free the conventional elements that may have stalled your leadership endeavour up until today. This idea will transform your orientation inside out, so that you become an elite force in understanding, and demonstration of exceptional leadership in any sphere.

On the other hand, if you perceive you know all that there is in this book, and perhaps much more. Yet, I encourage you to read as the uniqueness of communication and delivery of any knowledge, or information per time is perhaps the most crucial in learning. As this will further broaden your horizon so that your leadership capacity is enlarged, and refreshed with a new perspective to meet the challenges of now and the future. Thereby giving you advantage in our ever dynamic world.

> *The uniqueness of communication and delivery of any knowledge or information per time is perhaps the most crucial in learning.*

Afterall, in the words of Oprah Winfrey, *"the whole point of being alive is to evolve into the complete person you were intended to be"*. And I add by saying, knowledge learnt, unlearn, or relearn either through theory, observation or experience is a step in that direction of evolving into the real you.

Perhaps your prior mindset on leadership has been that leadership is a secondary endeavour, and so our natural selfish instinct is to respond with second class interest to any call to lead. But I make bold to say that, that is an erroneous standpoint. It may be the popular school of thought, but it is flawed. Leadership is not a secondary endeavour, neither is it a luxury. Leadership is not what you do after you have taken care of every other thing in your life. Leadership is primary to existence, it is the basic necessity to true living. Leadership is why you were created (Genesis 1:28). The mandate has been given to the real you, your spirit, and the deepest expression of you to lead as much as important as breathing is.

While grand stories of leadership endeavours are popular

when the subject of leadership is mentioned, (and of course such stories are featured in this book), you should also pay keen attention to the leadership lessons of seemingly not-so-grand stories of everyday lives of people that are easily overlooked. Reason is therein might be the most vital lessons that will determine your ultimate leadership engagement, influence and fulfillment. And I must quickly add here that you may not totally agree with some of the names, sources and brands mentioned in the course of this book, but you and I know that their leadership influence is undeniable.

First Thing's First

You cannot understand the true concept of leadership if you do not understand that leadership is spelt 'service'. I might end up confusing you the more by the time you finish reading this book, if you still think leadership is occupying a seat on a lofty position with arms folded, waiting to be pampered. This is totally incorrect!

In order to avoid messing up your comprehension on the subject of leadership. And not to be a disservice to you if I continue this masterpiece without telling you in plain terms, and in the simplest of language that leadership means service. It is not a position to occupy, but a disposition to engage, to make your creator proud, to make you better, and to influence your environment and world towards achieving a particular goal, objective or purpose.

So whenever you see the word "Lead" in this book, please replace with "Serve" in your understanding, and whenever you see the word "Leadership", kindly replace with the word "Service". Having established that, I think we can move forward now, and hope we will be on the same page all the way as regards that. But if you do not buy into this school of thought, you have not committed any offense if you discontinue reading this book. It may not just be for you.

On the other hand, if you have not always seen leadership from the perspective of service. However, if you are open and willing to welcome new ideas, either through testing and proving it to be true, or through other people's experience, thumbs up to you. And in this case, I urge you to test the idea that the whole essence of leadership is to serve. And as you take that step, this material will be a good resource for you to mirror the hypothesis.

LEADERSHIP IS PRIMARY TO YOUR EXISTENCE

Leadership is primary to the human existence, without it, we will go extinct in a short period. Without leadership, we will all be living on a time bomb.

The whole of human existence lends credence to leadership, the universe and all its elements point to this singular fact. If you do not lead, you break the natural rhythm of the universe, and add no value to life. And when you do not add value to life, you become stale, stink and a liability to both yourself, and your environment. Ultimately, you become an unprofitable investment to your creator. It is abnormal to the universe and the law of existence not to lead.

> *It is abnormal to the universe and the law of existence not to lead.*

Leadership is as important as the basic needs of human;

food, shelter, clothing and the likes.

The world has always revolved around leadership, knowingly or unknowingly, it is the base upon which every other thing exists.

It is not what you do out of convenience, but preparation is inevitable if you must excel at it. Just like an eagle is born to soar, it will however not naturally grow up to soar, it must go through the deliberate rigor and pain of learning to soar. The capacity to soar is potent in every eagle, but the reality of soaring comes with a price. And if an eagle is born and lives all its life among chickens, it might never know what it means to soar. The fact that leadership is a primary calling for us all, does not mean it will be a sweet, smooth and natural sail.

SOME ERRONEOUS MYTHS OF LEADERSHIP

MYTH 1: LEADERSHIP IS FOR THE SAKE OF OTHERS ONLY

An erroneous myth we have held so dear for ages is the notion that leadership is solely for the sake of others, when in fact, leadership is primarily a self-discovery and self-fulfillment endeavour. It enriches and blesses those who dare to step forward to lead first, before getting to the world around them. As stated earlier, this is not a conventional conviction. But let us see if this stand-point will eventually make sense or not.

Leadership is FIRST for YOU!

Leadership is first a primary endeavour because it first addresses the personal issues of the leader, before addressing that of his or her environment. It is an inside-out process. We will be digging deeper into this in the chapter that addresses this question of leading because of yourself.

However, let us take a quick example here; before you bought or were gifted this book, read and hopefully become better in your leadership walk; As the author, I have been greatly imparted positively in the process of birthing the book, more than I can ever imagine. The process exposed me to information that are mind shifting and character refining. And made me a more informed and prepared leader.

Furthermore, there is a new sense of responsibility to become a better leader that suddenly came upon me as a result of this project. Thus, this book has first transformed me, and made me a better leader before anyone else will get to have it. But all this I may never have known or experienced if I did not step out to offer my service in form of writing this book on leadership.

And very importantly, I want you to understand that leadership is not secondary to life endeavour as we know it. Leadership is primary to your existence, leadership is for you, and it is the bedrock of all human progress. Leadership is what gives meaning to humanity. You cannot live a meaningful life outside leadership. If you do not have a plan for leadership, then you do not have a plan for a true living. You can EXIST outside leadership, but you cannot LIVE outside leadership.

> *You can EXIST outside leadership, but you cannot LIVE outside leadership.*

Humanity is the primary tribe we all belong to, whether

you are black or white, we all are expressions of humanity, but humanity will lose its essence and steam without leadership. The reason is that humanity is not just a word standing on its own, it is a word or concept that is designed to add value and bless the world, and the only way humanity can bless the world, the channel and the engine or platform through which humanity can benefit the world is through leadership.

Your purpose discovery and fulfillment are locked in your acceptance and walking in leadership. The discovery of your purpose, and its fulfillment is tied to your resolve to lead because it addresses the reason for your existence, your uniqueness, gifts, talents, interests, experiences and even skills. It is your path to a maximum life.

Your purpose discovery and fulfillment are locked in your acceptance of leadership.

If you must live the life you were truly born to live,

If your life must matter on this side of existence,

If you must die fulfilling your dreams, release and maximize your potentials,

If you must breathe your last with no regrets whatsoever,

If you must live a life that adds value to your world,

If humanity must ever be grateful because you came to this world,

If you must live a life that honours the gift of life,

And if you must live a life that would make your creator's head swell with pride.

I urge you to WAKE UP, go through the rope and grinds of leadership, step out and step forward into leadership now!

Myth 2: Leadership is for the talented only

Another erroneous myth we have about leadership is that it is a thing for the talented only. First, it should be noted that we are all talented. But often times we used the word talented to refer to some obvious gifts, talents and skills like public speaking, singing, just to mention a few. But the truth is leadership goes beyond just your ability to speak well alone or display any of those obvious abilities.

All the innovations, breakthroughs in science and progress we have made in the world today are all fruits of leadership. Today, we can fly on a heavy metal equipment for a long distance at an incredible height in the sky because of leadership. I can talk to a brother in California, USA via a cell phone from the comfort of my room in Lagos, Nigeria because of leadership, just name it! All the progress you can think of. Whether in science, sport, medicine, technology, government, business, economy, culture, fashion, beauty, entertainment, and media, just to name a few, all give credence to the audacity of leadership.

Now if this is still a bit difficult to comprehend at this stage. I mean how does leadership really connect with all that is being mentioned above? Take a deep breath, and relax your nerves. As you follow on this journey of discovery in this book, your mind will expand so that you might end up more convinced than I am, that leadership is the last frontier, or better still, the only frontier of the human race. Keep in front of your mind that leadership is service coded.

MYTH 3: LEADERSHIP IS FOR THOSE IN TOP POSITIONS ONLY

Another erroneous belief about leadership is that, only the woman or man at the top is the leader. The man or woman that occupies the leadership position is qualified to be called the leader. This is a major belief that has hindered progress in our world, because we build system around this belief that end up paralyzing individual initiative that would have led to progress in any organisation or system. As much as the person at the top position of an organisation has a major role in determining the progress of any organisation, it does not remove your ability to serve and influence as a leader from whatever position you might be in the organisation.

True leadership however has little or nothing to do with position. Looking at our earlier definition of what leadership is about, there was no place where we refer to the position of a person, organisation, place or brand, but the disposition of the person, organisation, brand or place. You can serve and be influential without occupying any leadership position. Thus, you can be the lowest in an organisation and still be a leader, while on the other hand, you can be at the top position of an organisation, yet lack influence and the basic leadership qualities.

MYTH 4: LEADERSHIP IS FOR A PARTICULAR GENDER OR RACE

This is one of the greatest undoing in some parts of the world today, so that a productive percentage of their population is relegated to some certain level in the society due to their gender or race. And on the other hand, it has led to the extreme in another part of the world. Whereby in trying to prove wrong the relegation of one gender or race, it unconsciously or consciously lead to the victimization of the other gender or race.

On the gender issue, I believe men and women have their unique strength and abilities. This is obvious from way the they are built, talking about physical, emotional and otherwise, but none is less of the other when it comes to leadership dispositions, rather we should find point where one gender's uniqueness complements the other.

It is therefore an erroneous believe that one race or gender is superior to the other. And to choose a leader based on race or gender is the greatest undoing to any leadership endeavour. To choose a leader based on race or gender is a leadership engagement built on faulty foundation, and it will inevitably produce after its kind. There are statistics to prove this over and over again in every sector you can mention, from politics to economy, health, education, business, sports etc. that leadership is race and gender neutral.

While we address the various myths. On the other hand, we must understand that leadership is new thinking, leadership is innovation, leadership is value, and leadership is excellence, and those who innovate, those who inject new ideas into a system or process will always lead. Joseph's innovative idea in the Bible using technology to solve Egypt's agricultural crisis made him a prime minister.

If leadership is such an important idea, then it becomes inevitable that people, organisation, or brands must understand why they should lead per time. Therefore, this book uncovers and comprehensively address the X factor in leadership. The foundation of all worthwhile leadership endeavour; the question of WHY that puts everything in the right perspective. From knowing your WHY in any leadership engagement, to the three WHY(s) behind extraordinary leadership which is leading for your Creator, for yourself and for humanity.

If you do not lead, you break the natural rhythm of the universe and adds no value to life, and when you do not add value to life, you stink and become a liability to both yourself and your environment. Ultimately you become an unprofitable investment to your creator.

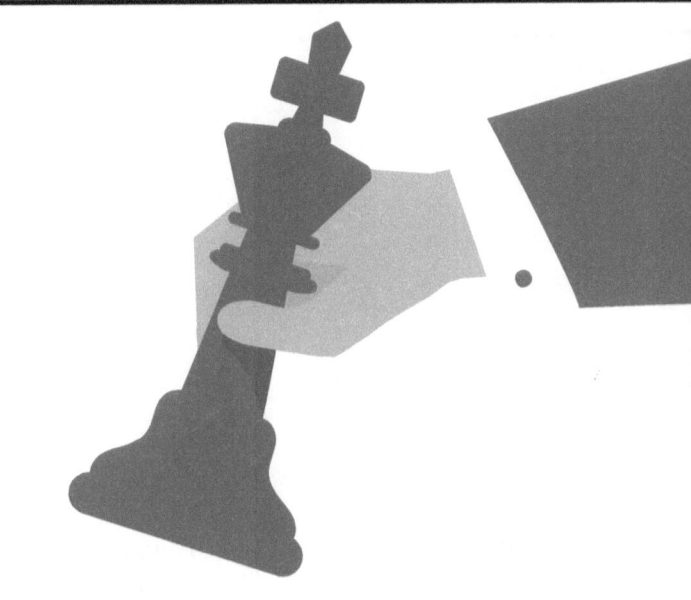

CHAPTER 2

Know Your 'Why'

THIS BOOK IS LONG OVERDUE BECAUSE IF YOU DO not know "why" you are doing what you do, you can be knocked down at the slightest challenge, and you have a 90% chance of doing it in error.

Yes, you can know "how" to do something, you can know the "what" in doing something or being something, and you can know the "where or when" in doing something or being something, but if you cannot answer the big question of "WHY" you should be something or do something, trust me you will be brought to your knees at the slightest opposition.

If you do not know "why" you do what you do, if your

"why" is not convincing enough to you, you will be knocked out of the ring of life every single day.

You can teach people all the skills, methods, strategies, and ways of leadership which you can find in 99% of most leadership books today, which is not bad though. In fact, I appreciate and am immensely grateful for the journey and work started, and commitment to the subject of leadership by all those before us. It is on their shoulders we are standing today to be able to dig deeper into this crucial subject. We are actually where we are today because of the amazing steps they have taken, and the immense work they have done. But all that will almost amount to nothing if we do not know why we should lead. If people do not know why they should lead, they will fizzle out sooner or later, because they are only leading from without, not within.

> *If people do not know why they should lead, they will fizzle out sooner or later, because they are only leading from without, not within.*

Leading from without is pleasing the society which is good,

but not enough reason to lead. Leading from without is doing it to please everyone else, not because you think it is the right thing to do, or you have a compelling reason. Sad to say here that if you do not know why you are leading, there are 99% chances you are leading from without, which is the popular convention in our world today. You can never be an authentic leader leading from without. Most of the leaders that have commanded the attention of the world in the past, are mostly leaders that consciously or unconsciously walk in this path of leading from within. Leading with an understanding of why you are leading. It is the truest, most authentic form of leadership that comes from nothing but within. It generates its energy from an immortal principle - the principle of 'why' with the infinite power that resides with the universe.

The principle of 'why' actually goes beyond the subject of leadership. It is the definition of any true course, and it is the test of any worthwhile endeavour. If you have not resolved your 'why' you are doing what you do in any endeavour, you will never hit the crescendo of satisfaction and fulfillment in that thing. Your ultimate happiness lies not in the amount of what you do, but in the conviction of the 'why' you are doing it. And it is funny to note that even if your 'why' is not true, but because you are convinced by that 'why', the entire universe will cooperate with you still. The world has always co-operated with the soul with the 'why'.

> *The principle of 'why' actually goes beyond the subject of leadership. It is the definition of any true course, and it is the test of any worthwhile endeavour.*

There will be an overriding 'why' at the core of your being that inspires you to lead. While every endeavour you engage in will come to demand its own 'sub-why' you should lead. Your overriding 'why' is what makes people entrust leadership position on you even with little knowledge about your capacity to lead in that particular endeavour. Your overriding 'why' is the spirit of leadership, it attracts responsibility to you regardless of your competence in the field you have been called to lead or not. It becomes intuitive to lead or assume you should lead. This has put many leaders into trouble as people suddenly think they are super humans that can do just about anything.

> *Your ultimate happiness lies not in the amount of what you do, but in the conviction of the 'why' you are doing it.*

DISTINGUISHED BY HER WHY

Prof. Dora Akunyili's name will continue to resonate not just in Nigeria, but the world over as she epitomizes a leader who understood, and had a firm grip on WHY she led so that she attained the status of an iron lady both home and abroad.

She was a Nigerian, an internationally renowned pharmacist, and former Director General of National Agency for Food and Drug Administration and Control (NAFDAC), the agency in charge of food and drugs regulation in her country, Nigeria. Her professional achievements, scholarship and commitment have been recognised over the years by many awards from organisations and governments in Africa,

Europe and America, including her nomination as one of the **'Heroes of our Time'** by Time Magazine in New York, and the **'International Service Human Rights Award'** which she received at the House of Commons in London.

Before she came to limelight, it will be great to feed you with her story of emergence as a trusted leader. In 1995 she was appointed secretary responsible for the distribution of funds to people in need by the Petroleum Trust Fund (PTF) where she suffered a stomach infection. With a sum of 25000 pounds, she was sent to London to be treated funded by the Federal Government of Nigeria. The English surgeon found that her infection was not serious and proposed to share her employer's funds. She refused and returned the money to her employer, the Federal Government when she got back to Nigeria. The story got out and the then president of Nigeria Olusegun Obasanjo heard about this. In 2001 she became the most suitable for appointment as head of the NAFDAC because of her precedent in PTF.

When she started her job, 62% of drugs were not authorised or approved, most of which were imported from China,

India or manufactured in a clandestine factory from somewhere such as Onitsha in the south of Nigeria, where the production of fake drugs is commonplace. Some of these "fake drugs" contained dangerous substances, others were a variant of the original product which has been diluted but their taste to remain the same. The loss of her sister to fake drugs while growing up, perhaps was the impetus for her WHY when she was called to lead the then most notorious and complicated sector of her nation at that time.

Contrary to her predecessors, she took her mission to heart and declared war on the "merchants of death". She limited drug imports to two seaports and two airports, she understood that it is not enough to fight the criminals here at home without taking the war to the beneficial companies outside Nigeria that form a fundamental aspect of the infamous trade; she used inspectors in China and India and blacklisted 31 manufacturers, taking action on 800 different accounts against specific sales and local production. She did not have to wait very long for their reactions, she was almost immediately offered one million dollars as a bribe to stop her actions. But not Prof. Dora Akunyili, her WHY for leading NAFDAC was too great to bend to any amount of hard currency.

When she refused the bribe, all hell was let loose, and they threatened her. So great was the violence and attempts at murdering her. Her son was the object of a kidnap attempt and then professional killers were sent after her. In one of the interviews she granted media, she narrated how her son escaped from attempted kidnap in school when he denied her, the kidnappers had asked if Prof. Dora Akunyili was his mother. This prompted her to send him to the US to join his siblings. While her children remained in the United States in the heat of the attacks, she stayed back in Nigeria to face the war squarely. And there was also the incidence of the burning of NAFDAC laboratory by these evil elements of fake drugs, while she waged war without mercy against the traffickers of fake drugs in Nigeria. On the 26th of December 2003 as she approached her home, her convoy was attacked, *"bullets shattered the back windscreen of my car, pierced my headscarf and burned my scalp like a hot water burn. A bus driver was killed on the spot."* She recalled.[1]

Prior to her assumption of office, Nigerians barely knew of NAFDAC's existence and its impact on its mandate was infinitesimal. In 2001, Nigeria had a high world record in counterfeit drugs, expired drugs and other unwholesome products which stood at about 70%; made in Nigerian drugs were banned in West African countries; the local pharmaceutical industry was in chaos: the local manufacturers faced declining fortunes while the foreign ones like Boots, ICI, and Sandoz closed shop and 90% of the packaged sachet water manufactured in the country were contaminated.

Under Dora's tenure, the picture dramatically changed. The Nigerian pharmaceutical industry returned to the path of growth and prosperity; the incidence of fake drugs fell to 20% in 2004 and 10% in 2006; the level of unregistered drugs declined from 68% in 2001 to 19 % in 2006, loaves of bread with potassium bromate nose-dived from 95% to 1%; sachets of packaged water became relatively safer, Nigeria was no longer a haven for expired or substandard drugs while Nigerian drugs became accepted in neighbouring countries. Paradoxically, regulatory officials from those countries that banned our drugs came to learn from NAFDAC in Nigeria while NAFDAC formed and led the campaign. In one of her campaign against fake drugs, Onitsha was raided and 700 policemen removed 80 truckloads of counterfeit drugs. [2]

While she fought external forces, she did not spare the internal as well in a bid to thoroughly clean the system, she took to shedding corrupt employees, getting rid of 300 members of staff over a period of six years (out of a total of 3000 people), including her brother-in-law which was one of those tough decisions she had to make for the ultimate good of her country. Committed and decided, she said, with tears in her eyes, *"False drugs, is the massacre of innocent lives and is a crime against humanity. We can protect ourselves against AIDS but we can do nothing against a deadly drug"*. And I would like to add to this quote that fake drugs can beat the most fortified security fortress to maim, kill and destroy anyone with no respect for VIP or ordinary citizens. [3]

During her 6 years tenure at the agency, she received

countless death threats, and survived several assassination attempts. Yet she engaged in a non-stop battle against fake drugs in her country. She was never scared to go on the offensive. She raised public awareness of the problem through campaigns and school competitions, she increased spot checks at sea and airports, and she publicly burnt fake drugs worth more than $150m. Also, the actions of the agency at a particular time led to 45 convictions and 60 pending court cases. [4]

So effective were her strategies that Nigerians even surrendered substandard products to NAFDAC for destruction on their own! Why and how did Akunyili succeed? Knowledge of the job: she had an incredible mastery of her area of expertise. Spoke and acted with intimidating confidence, passion and commitment for the job (and that was why she was not deterred by attempted assassination and death threats); she wept when the NAFDAC laboratory was burnt down and she used every opportunity to speak about her holy war on drug adulteration. People management: she was able to motivate, inspire and empower her staff to go for gold. Awareness:

she used the mass media to great advantage and succeeded in convincing Nigerians to shine their eyes whenever foods and drugs were concerned. All NAFDAC activities were made public including names, dates and figures.

Other reasons for her spectacular performance included compassion/consideration: she was considerate in handling those who fell short of NAFDAC's high standards. She explained why a given course of action was necessary, gave adequate notice before introducing new regimes and she dialogued directly with the stakeholders. Effective surveillance and enforcement: she used an ingenious mix of strategies in the pursuit of her holy war. She took the war to India and Pakistan from where most of the fake drugs were imported and brought the banks into the war. [5]

Having identified the areas above that sums up her Competence, Capacity, and Character to lead, one thing that stood out and gave her the last 'C' that made the difference was that Dora Akunyili was a woman that knew the 'WHY' behind her leadership of NAFDAC, and knowing 'Why' she led produced the last 'C' which is Courage. A leader can be competent, build capacity and have character, however, when he or she lacks courage, it will likely not last the test of challenging times and circumstances. It is only a leader that understand why she or he is in leadership that will find courage in the face of any opposition to push for progress or whatever it is they truly believe in.

Every human has the instinct and capacity for leadership, but most do not have the courage or will to cultivate it – Dr. Myles Munroe

Recalling one of the incidents that informed why she fought fearlessly, was about the fake insulin for diabetes which resulted in the death of her sister in 1988. She said, "not only was it fake and did not contain the insulin she was supposed to take, but it was also contaminated and gave her abscesses. She did not respond to antibiotics, AND WE JUST WATCHED HELPLESSLY UNTIL SHE DIED". [6]

I must however, emphasise here that Dora Akunyili's 'why' or story was not fueled by revenge but a call to take personal responsibility over what you do not like, a personal responsibility over thousands of children on the waiting list to die the same way her sister died. Great leaders they say are born in adversity; she was a perfect example. She was standing for something, for life, healthy life for all, and not only standing against the fake drug institutions and establishment.

Dora Akunyili and NAFDAC produced excellent results that amounted to miracles. After her sterling and unrivalled performance in NAFDAC, she went on to assume other leadership responsibilities in Nigeria. She was so legendary that she was appointed for positions outside of her primary sector which is health. [7]

Prof. Dora Akunyili remains one of Nigeria's brightest stars. Nigerians and the rest of the world whose lives she had touched directly or indirectly will never forget her legacy. Akunyili proved her versatility in different areas of human endeavour. Her local and international recognition and awards are over 800. After her demise, Dora's honours keep coming. She did not follow where the path may lead while serving her fatherland. Instead, she headed to where there was no path and left a trail at every government parastatal she ever worked in. Her memory and works can never be forgotten. Her legacies will continue to live with us; and will outlive us. The saying that, *"Great leaders do not set out to be leaders; they only set out to make a difference",* is apt describing only a few Nigerians like Prof. Dora Nkem Akuyili (OFR), former Director General of the National Agency for Food and Drug Administration and Control (NAFDAC). [8]

How much sacrifice you can make in any endeavour is dependent on your understanding of why you are doing it.

Today, start to lead from WITHIN, NOT WITHOUT and KNOW YOUR **'WHY'**.

If perhaps you did not know why you are doing something yet, now that you know how important it is, take time to ask questions, dig deep until you find the answer within you. It might not necessarily be a grand 'why', as some people might think because of the emphasis. Your 'why' may be as simple as the word 'simple' itself. For example, I wrote this book because I want to wake people up to the reality of the foundation to the subject of leadership.

But your 'why' at every point is of utmost importance because it will determine what you can take and what you cannot take in that endeavour. It will determine how much sacrifice you are willing to make for a cause. The people whose price tag you cannot negotiate are those who know the "why" behind their actions, decisions and indecisions. Your conviction is firm in any endeavour because your 'why' is clearly defined. In other words, your conviction in any endeavour is as strong as the 'why' you are doing it.

The people whose price tag you cannot negotiate are those who know the "why" behind their actions, decisions and indecisions.

In the same vein, the question of leadership without a clear definition or exposition on why people should choose leadership will not stand the test of time and be fully maximized if the "why" is not clear. Why you do what you do is more important than what you do, because when the chips are down, it is the only force that will keep you going. It will keep you walking when you have lost all your limbs, it will keep you flying when there are no wings, it will re-echo your voice when you have lost your speech, it will keep your vision even when you have lost your sight, it will keep you warm in the coldest of Arctic, it is the greatest of human unseen energy. It is what separates an ordinary soldier from an extraordinary soldier in any battle. Your 'why' in any situation is the heartbeat and lifeblood of your life's endeavour.

> *Why you do what you do is more important than what you do.*

However, there is a place for intuition at the start of venturing into something. Some people started a worthwhile endeavour without any significant 'why', but just mere instinct. Intuition can get you started on a particular cause, some of us were drawn into what we do now by 'mere' intuition. We never really had the sense of clarity we have now when we started. Personally, I have been engaged in worthy causes in my life only with the nudge from intuition, without having an idea of what it was, but a gut feeling just keeps nudging me in that direction. Something just tells me it is the right thing to do, without really having clarity.

For example when I started sharing daily prayer content with the Prime Time With God team on my Facebook account, and on instant messaging Apps like WhatsApp, I never really had an idea where it was leading. Yes, my objective was to bring God's presence to people, just the way I have enjoyed it by engaging the prayers daily, so it started on 'mere' instinct, but my perspective changed when it dawned on me that this was a ministry to reach out to people, and help them connect with God in an unconventional yet very intimate manner (especially for many like me who used to struggle with prayer because of the perception of God I grew up with), as the content of the prayer is often like a conversation with a friend. It is easier to have a conversation with a friend, where you can be real without no fear of condemnation. This simple understanding of the purpose it is meant to fulfil as a ministry changed the game for me.

Before the ministry episode, I used to be bothered about how many people liked it, how many responded to it, but when I got the insight that this was nothing but a ministry meant to fulfil a part of God's purpose in my life, my perspective about the exercise changed totally, my strength and encouragement no longer depended on people's reaction, responses, action or inaction, neither did anything external affect me, because, for the first time, the reason or the 'why' I should continue became internalized in me. This change of motive changed a whole lot for me. It changed my attitude about it, and from the day I saw it as a purpose-driven ministry, a new energy from within was engaged to do it as a priority. From that day, I stopped bothering about whether people will approve of it, or whatever the perception might be. Seeing it as a ministry gave me a purpose for doing it. It stopped from just being a show to a calling. Yes, it started with a 'mere' intuition but took purpose from discovering the 'why'.

So it is ok to begin on intuition. It is ok to stumble into

something with no clear purpose, but it is not ok to remain on intuition, there has to be a confirmation sooner or later as the reason behind your intuition. If not when challenges come, you are likely to find an escape route when the option provides itself. You can start a cause on intuition, but after a while, you need to know your 'why'. You need to know why you are doing it. You cannot maintain maximum energy on a course by 'mere' intuition.

In the same vein the question of 'Why" in leadership, why you should choose to be a leader cannot be overemphasized. Without a firm conviction of why you should be a leader which this book stands to clarify, your leadership journey will be defined and subject to conditions and environments, instead of the principles of leadership. Without answering the question of why, your leadership dispositions would be subject to compromise.

But remember, the world is doomed without leadership!

And no matter the amount of leadership already enjoyed by the world, your unique place in the scheme of things cannot be overlooked, the world will miss a significant note if you hesitate. Only you can deliver that note.

Africa has remained the underdog of the world for a very long time because she has refused to step up and step into leadership. The potentials are there no doubt, but leadership is greatly lacking.

Without 'your' leadership, or if you do not lead, you are ungrateful to God for the many potentials deposited in you. You will live below who you truly are, as you cannot maximize your life and potentials when you ignore leadership, and humanity will suffer for it, as your quota is withheld from adding its unique melody to the world's rhythm.

There are three "whys" of leadership comprehensively and precisely revealed in this book, the 3 that every other element of leadership rides on. No matter who you are, or where you are from, if you do not pay attention to this three 'whys' and fully embrace them, you have already set yourself up for failure and frustration. Beyond the issue of failure, leadership will not be inspiring to you. You will easily lose steam and the flavour of being a leader if you are oblivious of these three 'whys'.

Also, your interpretation and understanding of challenges in leadership would be clouded if you are ignorant of these three 'whys' of leadership. You can call it the powerhouse of any leadership endeavour.

Great leadership personalities recognized these three 'Whys' of leadership; **For God, For You and For Humanity.** Personalities like Steve Jobs, Dr. Christopher Kolade, Prof. Pat Utomi, Dr. Martin Luther King Jr., Nelson Mandela, Mother Theresa, Strive Masiyiwa, Elon Musk, Mahatma Gandhi, Chief Gani Fawehinmi, Prof. Dora Akunyili, Bill Gates, Denzel Washington, Angelina Jolie, Dr. Sam Adeyemi, Mark Zuckerberg, Jack Ma, Kola Oyeneyin and nations like Israel, US, UAE, China, Japan, Singapore etc., and organisations like Coca-Cola, Apple, Nike, Facebook, Google, Amazon etc. They all understand consciously or unconsciously the core message of the timeless truth in this book. And their responses to the three 'whys' of leadership has made them stand out of the pack. The three 'whys' which is For God, For You and For the World/Humanity.

Whether you are an individual, group of persons, organisation or brand, your true identity is in stepping into leadership. You must add your song to this uni-verse says Prince EA.

> *Whether you are an individual, group of persons, organisation or brand, your true identity is in stepping into leadership.*

The universe pauses, and pulses for the soul who knows their 'why', even when it is a stupid 'why'. The forces that engage the universe are not so concerned about how valid or credible your 'why' is. A man on a good cause without a 'why' can lose steam. While a man on a silly cause with a compelling 'why' will not only stand in the face of adversity, but the universe will conspire to stand with him.

A man on a good cause without a 'why' can lose steam, while a man on a silly cause with a compelling 'why' will not only stand in the face of adversity, but the universe will conspire to stand with him.

WHAT KEEPS LEADERS FOCUSED IS THEIR 'WHY'

Dr Nthabiseng Legoete is a medical practitioner who is passionate about improving access to primary health care. Motivated by her faith and own family story, her vision was to make quality primary healthcare affordable for all global citizens in emerging markets. To this end, Legoete founded QualiHealth in Johannesburg, South Africa. [9]

QualiHealth is a privately incorporated South African company built around the provision of affordable, convenient, high quality, world-class health care for individuals that may be employed but cannot afford private healthcare and expensive health insurance. Due to a range of complex factors, such individuals are not always able to get full value from public health facilities and would be willing to pay for affordable healthcare. They are often described as being in the "bottom of the pyramid" or the "excluded middle". Their plan was to provide effective primary health care to this segment in South Africa in the short term and Africa and other emerging markets in the medium to long-term. They were able to achieve affordable world-class healthcare through a judicious application of innovation in the overall philosophy to healthcare service provision. [10] Currently serving more than 600 patients a day at four facilities, in 2018 they are expected to grow to 30 facilities.

Dr Nthabiseng Legoete's life story thus far has, therefore - in a big way - influenced and contributed to her opening QualiHealth with the urgency that she had. On July 28, 2015, her uncle died. He had been ill for a month and was going to the clinic complaining of fatigue, all they gave him was vitamin B tablets. He eventually developed shortness of breath and contacted her. He lived quite far from her and by the time she intervened, he was at a stage of critical heart failure. He needed ICU intervention and subsequently died. [11]

Dr Legoete shared her story at the Global Leadership Summit (GLS) 2018, emphasizing that leaders must stay focused on why they started any cause they have embarked on. It is knowing why you are leading or why you are doing what you do, that will keep you focused in the midst of challenges, because challenges are part of a purpose-filled journey regardless of what informed your vision in the first place. According to her, life is really hard for the typical resident of Diepsloot, South Africa, and inadequate healthcare compounds the problem. Residents there do not have adequate access to even basic health care services, and there is a high prevalence of treatable diseases like tuberculosis and HIV. There are only two public health clinics, and they do not have the capacity to serve the people. To add to this, the closest referral hospital from Diepsloot is nearly 40 kilometres away (approximately 25 miles). [12]

Leaders who know their 'why' will remain focused in the face of challenges.

She knew there was a need for an urgent intervention. She had been privileged to work as a doctor in both the private and public sectors and understood the challenges of both. She was faced with the inefficiencies and bad service that you receive in the public sector. Her experience in the private sector was completely different; it ran like a well-oiled machine. It was well resourced, and it was efficient. However, it was not accessible to everybody. The good healthcare service was only accessible to about 18% of South Africa's population. [13] Her family incidence and the situation in her community informed the strong foundation behind why she does what she does, and it has helped her stay focused as a leader despite the challenges.

According to Dr Legoete at GLS 2018, there is a tendency to say "this does not work," when faced with a challenge like she did for a while, but focusing on why you started will shut out the 'noise' that causes distraction. Challenges do not mean that the dream is not working. Challenges are what they are; stepping stones to move you to a greater place. Therefore, you must be flexible on how you get to your goal. Changing the HOW does not mean that we change the WHAT or the WHY. Collaborate with those in alignment. Disassociate from parties that are misaligned. Be unwavering in what you want to achieve. *"We had too many people who were not helping us get to the goal. We had inflated costs that did not make sense. Most of those costs were associated with people who were not leading us to our goal."* She added. [14]

And the 'why' behind your leadership or service endeavour will help you realize and understand that it is not about you, so what people say or think will not mean much in pursuit of your goal. A leader cannot excel when he or she is trapped in how people are thinking of them, it is just noise. You do not worry over whether people like you or not as long as that is not the reason behind the cause you embarked on. Every leader goes through pain, but when you encounter pain and challenges show them your 'why'. And on why she kept at her goal despite the criticisms, and which she gladly shares whenever there is an opportunity, this was her response, *"If we are able to stand and take the criticism without being deterred, maybe we can encourage others."* – Dr Nthabiseng Legoete. [15]

Her last thought in the videocast at GLS 2018 is so apt that it captures the core of not just this chapter but this book when she ended by saying, *"Are you achieving? Are you doing what you set out to achieve, and if you are doing that, everything else is just noise, so when next you meet me in a year, in two years, in two months, however long, what will be unwavering and unchanging about me is that I want to democratize health care, I definitely would have changed how I achieve that, but what would have not changed is the WHY I started, and WHY I would continue on this journey".*

The universe pauses, and pulses for the soul who knows their 'why'.

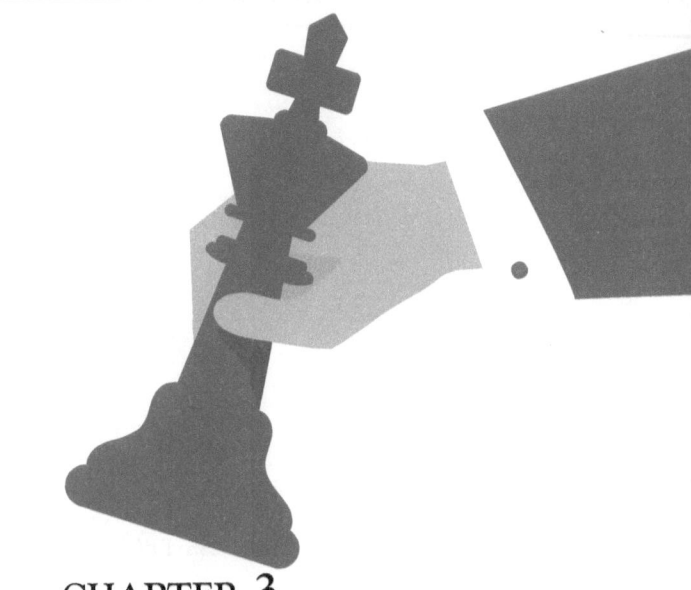

CHAPTER 3

LEAD FOR GOD

IT WILL BE A FRUITLESS EFFORT TO TRY AND DEFINE God in the most accurate and contained way. And you might have a different opinion about who God is which is ok, but the only idea that best establish God here in my own perspective is in John 1:3 in the scripture. In the simplest but classic of statement, it says, *'Everything was created through Him; nothing – not one thing! – came into being without Him.'* This statement succinctly lays the background to this chapter, the reason for God being the first 'why' you should lead. There are many references to the source of humanity, but I can only share the one that resonates with me through a proven conviction beyond any doubt. So all through this book, like you have noticed already, you will see references to this conviction.

Your first reason why you should and must lead is to show appreciation to the immense, unlimited and unfathomable potentials deposited in you even before you knew it. A special Grace that was given you by God before you were born physically. If you do not believe in God, you at least appreciate nature, and believe in the immense blessing of nature and her immeasurable investment in you. Being that as it may, the potentials however, will remain in a raw and unproductive form if you do not exercise it in the place of leadership, in the place of expression of this innate infinite power inside you, and the place of taking responsibility in service.

The God of creation has deposited His gifts among men and women, some He gave administration, some management, some songs, some books, some the sky to conquer, some the sea, some nature to tame, to some He gave special kind of wisdom, some words, some entertainment, some in making merry, some encouragement, some makeup, some fashion, some beauty, some buildings, some cuisines, some structure, order and governance, some systems, some critical thinking, some accounting, some technology, some literature, some imagination, some innovation, some ideas, the list of His deposit are endless, with many having more than one, and you can bear witness to that.

Kindly add yours here .... if it was not mentioned or you have others that were omitted.

Your talents, gifts and potentials are the primary triggers of the leadership potentials in you, simply because leadership is service which rides on adding value through your gifts, talents, passion, strengths and abilities. And these gifts and uniqueness were given to you by the God of creation. So don't you think He deserves a good bargain for His investment?

Leadership is when that unique gift finds expression, they were not given to be kept under your duvet and cuddle like two lovebirds in honeymoon.

We have over 7 billion people in the world as at the time of this publication, and no one soul is exactly like you. Can you beat that? Yes you have heard it before that you are unique, but I am affirming it here again that you are unique. It is not a cliché, if everybody has been deceiving you by telling you that, trust me I have no business whatsoever joining them to deceive you, I do not even know you so why should I get you excited unnecessarily, even if I know you, sorry I am too busy for that. Again I say, you are unique and you need to release your unique flavour to the world through leadership.

It will be a bad business for God, or Mother Nature would have shortchanged herself, as a venture that is not viable if you do not make use of the leadership potentials in you. This is the first reason why you should be a leader, because leadership is giving via service, giving what you have been given to the benefits of others. Leadership is meant to give expression to your potentials, gifts, passion, likes, interest etc. The place of appreciating God for the gift of leadership is in expressing it, and it is in the place of expressing it to bless the world that you find purpose.

The place of appreciating God for the gift of leadership is in expressing it, and it is in the place of expressing it to bless the world that you find purpose.

As we are different, so are we born with diverse gifts that will give us the advantage and audacity to lead a new and unique cause in our life's endeavour. But we need the courage to accept our uniqueness, to embrace it, to work it out and to maximize it, regardless of any opposition that may arise.

You cannot truly say you are a grateful soul if you do nothing with your talent, and you cannot truly lead without engaging your talent. Anyone that must lead, must do so from a point of strength, passion, deepest interest, intuition and natural flow, wherein lies everyone's infinite power. Leadership that will resonate with your followers must come from the point of your passion and essence.

Leadership that will resonate with your followers must come from the point of your passion and essence.

The parable of the talents in the Bible whose master gave his stewards varied measures of talent is a great example of what it meant to lead from what you have, and the consequence of not putting to use your talent or rather your creator's gift to you. The master's ultimate fulfillment was not in how much he was going to get from their trade, but in the expression of Himself through the talents He gave, this is why he insisted the one with one talent should have deposited his talent in the bank, which would have yielded some interest at least.

Barrister Ige Adelayo is a friend and a leader I have come to respect her leadership disposition. She shared with me a story of how this resonated with her in an event that happened a while back. She believes it is a privilege to serve and agrees that leadership is indeed service to GOD first, before any other thing. And she added something very profound which is not considered much today, and that is leadership starts from where you are, sometimes in a split moment of decision, and if we are not prepared, sensitive and careful enough, we can miss the best opportunity to lead.

It was her first time in the city of Ilorin, Nigeria, and she barely knew her way around the town. She was fresh out of National Youth Service Corps (NYSC) camp located at Yipata in Ilorin. NYSC is an initiative by the government of Nigeria to engage graduate from higher institutions under certain age to serve their fatherland for one year, in various sectors of the economy in a region of the country different from their origin. This is an attempt by the government to integrate the different regions of the country

And on this particular day when she came to open an account for her monthly allowance at Taiwo, a place in Ilorin. As she stepped out of the bank, she listened carefully for a cab going to Tanke (a place in the city of Ilorin) and observed that as cabs going to Tanke and other destinations arrived, people rushed, shoving each other if necessary, to board them and she was not quite sure where to start from. It was in the midst of all of this that she noticed a lady, a slightly plump, light-skinned trying to catch a cab as well. She sat on a wheelchair, unaccompanied, trying her best to compete for the cabs with the other pedestrians who kept outrunning her.

Ige listened and observed carefully to enable her to ascertain the lady's destination. A few seconds after, she saw a cab going to the lady's destination and before she realized it, she found herself behind her with a quick hello and a friendly smile, she wheeled the lady as fast as she could in the direction of the cab, although they missed that cab by the hair of a whisker, she successfully got her on the next cab that was going her way. She also opened the cab boot and placed her wheelchair in it without any support. Putting a smile on the lady's face.

"This story has not left me all these years because of the lessons I learnt from it. I learnt that strength and power come in the place of service. Anyone who knew me well at that time of my life (I was really skinny and fragile) will know that I could not have pushed the lady on the wheelchair and outrun several people, let alone carry her pure metal wheelchair by myself." Ige recalled. The truth is something in her knew that she had to do something to help the lady. That is what Dr Myles Munroe described as the Spirit of Leadership.

When she finally outran the other people at the bus-stop and yanked open the car door, it seemed as if they suddenly realized that they ought to have shown her preference, they all paused for her to complete her task, although they did not help with the chair. Some assumed that she knew the lady and was going with her but later discovered that was not the case. As she did not join her. Another lesson I learnt from Ige's story is that in the midst of the chaos and madness going on around us and in the world, people are yet looking for who will take the initiative and lead to make things right! She is inclined to believe that someone learnt a lesson that day.

On the other hand. On her part instead of choosing to serve and put the lady's needs before hers, she could have analyzed the situation and concluded that:

a. It is not her job and she does not know her;

b. She was not going the lady's way and blame people going her way for their insensitivity;

c. She was physically too weak for the task (which would have been true based on her history with lifting heavy objects) and;

d. The government is to be blamed for not being sensitive to the needs of physically challenged citizens.

All these are completely genuine reasons not to help the

lady on the wheelchair, but the call to leadership trumps the excuses and made the difference at the end.

The decision she took to serve the lady was a decision to serve God and she was given strength for the task. Beyond this, she recalled that she experienced very uncommon help and assistance throughout her time in Ilorin, Nigeria where she did her NYSC, the kind that was very instrumental to her career and future years down the line. She sincerely believe that there is a link between that day's event and the numerous testimonies of benefits she experienced in that city, and she has seen this principle reoccur several times in her leadership experience which makes her conclude; *"Every time we have an opportunity to lead by serving (formally or informally), it is an opportunity from God to bless us and use us to bless people as we honour Him with our servant leadership."* She added.

WE REPRESENT OUR CREATOR THROUGH OUR LEADERSHIP DISPOSITIONS

When we create a product or service, we have an expectation of what the product should meet, we have an objective in mind, and we want the product to fulfil the purpose for its creation. No business or organisation just create a product or service without considering the above mentioned. We want it to meet the need for which it was created. And when it does not meet this expectation, often times we become unhappy. What our product or service does, or the need it meets is more or less our greatest reward for creating such a product or service. In the same vein, this is what our expression of leadership or service means to our creator.

On this side of existence, we represent the little expression of the higher being that controls the universe. It is an established fact that we are gods here on earth stemming from the conversation that ensued prior to our creation, points to this fact. In Genesis, the idea of creating you was thrown to the heavenly council, when it was said, "let's make man in our own image and likeness". And so our duty here is to give credence to this fact. You are not your own. You are a product of a community, a heavenly community, and you are gifted with infinite power in form of talents, gifts, passion and other manifestation of your unique strength.

Your gift, talent and abilities were given to you by God to

bless the world, and they can only find expression when you step out and lead. The greatest leaders we celebrate today had this in common. They had talent, ability, capability and experience, and they stepped out and led. Your gift to God is your expression of these infinite power. When you express your gift at the place of leadership, you allow God speak to the world through you.

Have you noticed that growing up that our parents are always mad when they discovered we know something about a subject in school, and yet we decide not to provide them answer to it when we are being asked to, perhaps because we were shy at that point. They just cannot seem to understand, why we will have an answer to a problem, and yet decide not to recommend it when needed. In fact, most times, parents are happier about what you make out of life based on who you are, and the family you represent, than what you do for them. What you do with your life is their greatest reward not necessarily what you do directly for them. If it is in you, they expect you to express it, if they have invested in you, they expect you to express it.

Most parents do not mind how much they pay for their

children's school fees so long as they can afford it, they are more concerned when there is no evidence of such investment in the child. So you should lead because a lot has been invested in you by the God of creation, do not waste the investment. To whom much is given, much is expected, and much has been given to everyone, whether you believe it or not, we will not dwell on that now, that's probably another topic for another day.

You should engage your gift, skills and experience to lead because you have been given for expression. Take note of the word 'skills', which you are not necessarily born with, but you have been given the capacity from birth to house the seed of whatever skills you will ultimately develop. Your body has the property to carry whatever skills you will eventually develop, even though they were not initially there when you were born.

Leadership is simply your responsibility and gift to God who created you unique with potentials the world needs.

This is why organisations whose potentials are high in use, are usually referred to as "the leading so and so organisation"

You must understand that your first purpose of leading is to be a worthy ambassador of your creator because you have been given so much. You must deliver that which your 'home country' or host has assigned you with. Therefore, your first reason or your first 'why' in leadership is because you have been endowed by God to come here and empty yourself for the good of humanity, so the greatest appreciation of your endowment is to lead, because in leading you release and maximize your potentials.

There is an expectation of a student from Harvard, Stanford, Yale, MIT, Oxford, Cambridge, and a couple of other Ivy League universities, because of the investment that has gone into them. In the same way, there is a high expectation on you, consciously or unconsciously. Even when nobody bothers you. Yes, nobody may have an idea of what has been deposited in you, nobody may truly be able to tell what you have been given, what exactly you carry on the inside, but your intuition knows, and will continue to nudge you to wake up to your true self. The higher life, the life you were truly born to live, the life of leadership, or rather exceptional leadership through service. You will never be satisfied, and you will remain a restless soul until you obey this higher calling. *"For the creation earnestly waits for the manifestation of the sons of God.* So boldly affirms the great book.

Leadership is a Mandatory Call

You cannot delay anymore, they say delay is dangerous and that is very true. Do not sleep when you are being counted on. Do not defer when it is your turn to strike your part of the orchestra note, even if you have only been given one string instrument in the whole of the orchestra band, without your single note, it will not be complete, so do not defer. Do not break the rhythm. Wake up and lead!

Do not defer when your service is needed at home,

Do not defer when your service is needed abroad,

Do not defer when your service is needed to save a life,

Do not defer when your service is needed to bring happiness and laughter to people,

Do not defer when your service will cause people to emerge,

Do not defer when the key to redemption is in your hands,

Do not defer…

What if Harriet Tubman had deferred?

What if Mahatma Gandhi had deferred?

What if Mother Theresa had deferred?

What if Mao Zedong had deferred?

What if Martin Luther king Jr. had deferred?

What if Lee Kuan Yew had deferred?

What if Nelson Mandela had deferred?

What if Sam Adeyemi had deferred?

What if Michael Jackson had deferred?

What if Jeff Bezos had deferred?

What if Michael Jordan had deferred?

What if Mohammed Ali had deferred?

What if Kanu Nwankwo had deferred?

What if Kola Oyeneyin (Mr. SleevesUp) had deferred?

What if Strive Masiyiwa had deferred?

What if Mark Zuckerberg had deferred?

What if Steve Jobs had deferred?

What if Oprah Winfrey had deferred?

What if Bill Gates had deferred?

What if Dr. Stella Ameyo Adadevoh had deferred?

What if Lebron James had deferred?

What if Malala Yousafzai had deferred?

What if Atunyota Akpobome (Ali Baba), Nigeria's King of Comedy had deferred?

What if the Wright Brothers had deferred?

What if Abraham Lincoln had deferred?

What if Thomas Edison had deferred?

What if TD Jakes had deferred?

What if the Men That Built America had deferred?

What if Chief Gani Fawehinmi had deferred?

What if Sheik Mohammed Bin Rashid Al Maktoum had deferred?

What if Tyler Perry had deferred?

What if Prof. Dora Akunyili had deferred?

What if Magic Johnson had deferred?

And what if Jesus Christ had deferred?

What about brands and organisations;

What if Apple had deferred?

What if Google had deferred?

What if General Electric had deferred?

What if Facebook deferred?

What if Nike had deferred?

What if Amazon had deferred?

The list you know is endless.

And if this book has added value to you so far. What if the author had deferred in writing it?

Think about it.

You cannot say you are truly grateful to God for the immense leadership potentials in you, if you do not step out and lead. The Giver of the gift wants to express it here, and you are that vehicle of expression. Know from this day that anytime you express yourself in leadership, God is actually being expressed. Every time you serve someone, The Creator is happy because that is the only form he can reach people physically.

Therefore, the call to leadership is not actually optional. It is not about how you feel or how you do not feel, because it is not all about you. There is a grand plan somewhere. The evidence of that grand plan lies in your uniqueness. The evidence to the fact that you are called to lead lies in the fact that you are different. That is why you are not exactly like everyone else, even if you are born identical twins. So you can not relinquish your duty to another. You are different for a reason. The Creator is at loss every time you relinquish your place to lead. All the heavenly host weep when you fail to lead. It is a double tragedy when you have a star-studded team who are underperforming, not because they do not have the capacity, but because they just do not see the need to perform regardless of the investment. You know such situation can drive anyone insane.

The evidence to the fact that you are called to lead lies in the fact that you are different.

Saying no to the call makes you a fugitive, if I must put it in the most diplomatic term. But it is a more grievous crime than that. It is a crime against God, against yourself because you shortchange your opportunity to be a better person, and against humanity.

We cannot afford to waste resources. Step out and lead because God made you for that purpose. God is the first beneficiary when you step up to leadership. You make him a good investor by being a leader, because in leadership you maximize your potentials.

Remember, if YOU do not utilize what you have been given in the place of leadership, no one else can use it the way you will. Even if someone else has a prototype, it will yet lack your uniqueness. Sadly, but true.

Do not be an ungrateful soul. It is against the rhythm of creation, and the system that makes the world go round.

Now, lead!

CHAPTER 4
LEAD FOR YOU

No man or woman can truly live a fulfilled life, without first answering the call to leadership. And paying the price of leadership in any capacity. No matter how much you think you know yourself, you cannot truly come to the knowledge of your full capacity if you have not been x-rayed, and stretched by the demand of leadership.

When you do not let your leadership potentials to be fully expressed, you become like a stagnant water. And because you are not maximizing your potentials, you become toxic to yourself and the world. A stagnant water is useless to itself and the environment.

Against popular convention, the second beneficiary when

you accept leadership after your creator is not people, but you. It is in leadership, you give expression to your true self. It is in leadership you engage your gifts, talents, skills, passion and experience for the benefit of others, but it starts with you and from you.

It is because you even have an offer in the first place, before you can reach out to the world with any offer. You cannot give what you do not have. You having it is the first stage, and that is primary to leadership.

It is because you even have an offer in the first place, before you can reach out to the world with any offer.

Therefore, the call to leadership should thrill you. It should get you excited, perhaps super excited, because it is first a call to identify with your content. And to be a person of value to yourself, which makes you an important and valuable person. If you do not have anything, you cannot give anything and you cannot be of value to anyone. Most times, I encourage that you do not lose sleep, or bother yourself so much about where to deploy your leadership because when you become a person of value, the world sees it and are drawn to it. Your natural place where you are needed will gravitate towards you. And when it calls, please do not break the rhythm. Follow where the path leads fearlessly and courageously.

You cannot successfully lead anybody if you have not first led you, yourself. The process of you trying to get better in whoever you are, or whatever you do with the intention to add value to others ultimately makes you a better person. Like I mentioned at the beginning, before anyone will eventually get this book, read and hopefully become better in their leadership walk. I have been greatly imparted positively in the process of birthing the book, more than I can ever imagine. The process exposed me to information that are mind shifting, and character refining. These are information I may not have known but for the fact that I decided to serve my world with a book on leadership. Most of which are inspired information because of my mindset, as well as my experience and those of others. Furthermore, there is a new sense of responsibility to become a better leader that suddenly came upon me as a result of this project. Thus, this book has first transformed me the author, imparted me with timeless leadership insights, and made me a better leader before anyone else will get to have it. But all this I would never have known or experienced if I did not step out to offer my service by writing this book.

The process of you trying to get better in whoever you are, or whatever you do with the intention to add value to others ultimately makes you a better person.

This is why vision-driven organisation take time to train people. They take time to develop their team. Especially when people attain the new position in such organisation, because they understand that every position comes with a new challenge that can only be solved with new capacity. They understand clearly this principle of being a better person to yourself, before you can be a better person to others.

This second reason or why you must lead should really excite you because now we are talking about you! Yes, you!

The belief or mindset that the sole purpose for leading is because of people, wear down many great leaders. It puts too much unnecessary pressure on anyone leading, causing them to become fatigued. It can be greatly exhausting when all you think about is how to satisfy others. If all the reason you do what you do is because someone else must be pleased, even though it comes with its own unique sense of fulfillment, you can easily wear out. More so when we live in a world where people have tendencies to become ungrateful of leaders and their efforts.

In fact, this is one of the reasons why many leaders today are lonely and depressed. The pressure to satisfy, please and impress others. The pressure to always perform better than your last gig, without taking much time to savour the moment, and be grateful for where you are, who you are or who you are becoming. This can really be a lonely path for leaders, as the society's expectations of you keep rising. And leaders are scared to be seen as vulnerable, because the society gives you a body language that confirms the fact that you are not going to be spared as a leader if you make mistakes. You must be on your best behaviour 24/7. Regardless of what you are going through. No matter what you have done in the past, no matter how great your last performance was, because people have short memory.

In leadership, there are people who are impossible to please but you must strive to do your best anyways. A lot of leaders have battled with depression at one time of their lives. While some are silently battling with depression, and they cannot cry out because they do not want to be seen as vulnerable. They are supposed to be looking out for everyone else but themselves.

Man (humanity) is essentially a spirit being, and the nature of a person's spirit dictates the nature that he or she manifests. Until a person's spirit is changed, the person is unchanged. Leadership, therefore, begins in the spirit of a person. When the spirit of leadership comes alive, it produces an attitude that separates the leader from the follower. – Dr Myles Munroe

---

And to a very large extent, their predicament stems from this erroneous mindset, a perspective or a narrative that says, your primary purpose for leadership is for others.

Living to perform for others, to wow them even when you are dying, to always command their accolades no matter the cost. This is good in itself, but when it becomes the sole reason for leadership without any attention to the need and the betterment of the leader, we miss the point. Which leaves most leaders miserable when the applause is over, because at that point their identity is defined by how good they perform, not who they really are without the performance. Some leaders end up being useless to themselves after leaving leadership position.

THE BIRTHING OF THE SPIRIT OF LEADERSHIP

I have always been fascinated and drawn to leadership. Many times I have experienced leadership responsibility entrusted to me even without knowing why. In most instance people believe I have the capacity to lead, and should lead. Whether it turned out well or not, the passion that I commit is undeniable. This is noticed by people most times without my knowledge, and prompted their recommendation.

But I took a back seat when I gained admission into the University of Lagos, Nigeria. I did not take the call to leadership seriously or very seriously. One of my reasons for being laid back was because I thought no extracurricular activity was worth my time, especially being a not-so-young student in the university. This trend continued until an event in the university disrupted this mindset. This event sparked the 'why' in me so that I began to see leadership or service as an all-important mandate.

I have had more than one moment of truth in leadership, many episodes of epiphany, and many revelations on leadership. Moments that stir up the nudge to lead. Some with mentors, role models and others with everyday people or event. I have also had accumulations of unremembered moments, sometimes a word said in passing that births or keep nurturing the spirit of leadership in me. One of such defining moments was in the university.

My experience with Fela Durotoye birthed in me what Dr. Myles Munroe referred to in his book (The Spirit of Leadership) as a Unique Mental Attitude called the Spirit of Leadership. It is what sits at the core of why great leaders led the way they did.

Sometimes in the year 2010, not quite sure of the exact date now, while I just newly got into school. It was during one of those lineup of activities to welcome fresh students into the university environment, to onboard them into campus life, and to hint them about life after campus.

Before now, the name Fela Durotoye had been flying around. And I had come to know him as one passionate Nigerian. As a passionate Nigerian myself, it was easy to connect with his ideas and thoughts.

As a fresher, I went to almost all the orientation programmes. Both the ones organized by the school management, and the ones organized by the various church fellowships. However, my motive for attending the ones organized by fellowships was not really because of the content of what I am going to take away from the knowledge that will be shared. But the underlying motivation was the snacks, gifts and souvenirs that will be shared. So because of this, I literarily attended all the orientation programs organized by the various fellowships.

And on this particular day, during one of the school's orientation event at the university's main auditorium. There was an instruction that all fresh students should endeavour to attend the program. Myself and a large number of my course mates, who later became friends headed for the main auditorium. And there was a man called Fela Durotoye speaking. I am not quite sure what his topic was, but I can remember how his speech made me feel. A passionate speaker with great content. And on this stage, doing what he knew how to do best; shaping lives with his undiluted truth, full of compassion.

He talked about leadership, and drove it home with the need for a new breed of leaders in Nigeria. In rounding up, he made what is similar to what is called 'altar call' in church. But in this case, it was for those who were willing and ready to serve in various leadership capacities, to come to the front as he was led to pray and commissioned them into leadership.

A lot of students came out, full of excitement and in the euphoria of the high spirit in the hall. Perhaps 70 percent of people from the fully-packed main auditorium of the University of Lagos came to the front, to be commissioned into leadership by this man who has painted the picture of a new Nigeria to us.

Full of excitement and with a conviction that cannot be uttered, I joined the rest of the students to be blessed by this phenomenon of a man. And then the most amazing thing happened when he said, *"If you know you are going to embezzle or steal money in leadership at any level after this prayer, I am going to lay a curse on you. So if you do not trust yourself very well. Or you are not very sure if you will embezzle or misappropriate funds in any leadership capacity. Kindly and quietly go back to your seat, because I am going to lay a curse on you now if you do"*. Now I am not sure if to say I expected what happened next after this audacious proclamation by Fela. But the number of students that went back to their seats was so immense that those who stood their ground were a microscopic few.

It was a great test for me, so that even some close course mates went back to their seat as well. Some even giggled and whispered to me while leaving to think twice about it. But somehow, maybe Grace made me stand my ground before this man that had sold a dream to me. While standing there, I struggled, because he kept begging that if you are not sure of your way with funds in leadership. Kindly go back to your seat. It was the most challenging few minutes of my life. He has said clearly and boldly he was going to lay a very disastrous curse on whoever steals money in leadership among us. My body quaked with uncertainty in those few minutes that looked like hours.

I cannot tell you my deepest conviction for not backing out, but somehow I knew this is where I belong; among the Eagles, those who will not bow or compromise their standards regardless of whatever test will come their way. One thing was sure, I knew I will forever be miserable if I back out, not because of what anyone or everyone will say, because truly at that moment, backing out was the comfort zone. It was the coolest thing to do. In fact remaining in front was the oddest thing in the world. But for me, backing out was like selling my birthright. It was like distorting the harmonious rhythm at the core of my existence and being. So with the little nerve, I had left I stood. At this time, I could count the students that remained in front, we were very few. Just a handful.

While we were trying to recover from the shock of what

was going on, the biggest surprise happened. An event that will forever remain with me. A lesson that reverberates to the very core of my existence. As we were standing waiting for him to lay the curse on whoever steals money when they gets to leadership position, this genius of a leader said, *"now I am NOT going to lay a curse on you, because you stood your ground for what is right. I will no longer lay a curse on you. And I will even pray that if peradventure you embezzle or misappropriate funds, that the mercy of God will deliver you, and make a way of escape for you to do what is right. And you will not be destroyed for it."*

Trust me, this brought me to tears. I wept because it was an experience that taught me a deep lesson. An experience I will never ever forget. I have learnt a lot when it comes to leadership, from books, people, observation and experience, but never in this dimension. It brought me to my knees appreciating the Grace that made me follow my intuition that day. After that experience, my mindset on leadership became that of mission. My confidence to succeed in any leadership endeavour skyrocketed. I knew forces beyond me were always there for me when I assumed any leadership platform. I am more than sure of succeeding in leadership because that experience was my official commissioning into leadership. It was a deeply spiritual experience, a mental, intellectual, character test that reverberates around my entire being, touching the core of my existence. I CAN NEVER FORGET. This happened years back, but it is just like yesterday.

And the testimonies from friends, family, colleagues, acquaintance and not-so-friendly fellows on my humble leadership walk so far, as a result of this singular act and many other events as stated earlier, has continued to increase, from student leadership to my experience in NYSC, in the various teams I have led in organisations, and serving as volunteer in various platforms. To this day, the testimonies has remained that I have never lacked vision, ideas, creativity, direction or the power of imagination in any leadership endeavour. This experience with Fela Durotoye is beyond a lifetime. That day I learnt how to stand for what I believe, even when it is not a popular opinion. I learnt what it means to be a non-conformist. I learnt to live the only life I have been called to. The only life I have been bequeathed capacity by providence; a life of service, truth of conviction, purpose, passion, integrity, and excellence. I have encountered great challenges in my leadership journey. Many times I have fallen on my face, I have been greatly persecuted and misunderstood, I have made mistakes, I have acted foolishly, I have underestimated the power of love in leadership and overrated vision, I have doubted my potential to lead, I have failed many times, and regretted greatly in some instances, but I have come out of it all shining bright like a diamond after every unpleasant experience because of this encounter with Fela Durotoye and many other experiences. It birthed the willpower, right mindset, stamina, and grace for leadership in me.

I do not boast of a perfect leadership engagement as I am still a work in progress, but I have exuded leadership dispositions that amazes people just being true to myself. Gets them talking and organically pouring positive encomium, while I try not to lose my head in encomiums.

The sense of being prepared, ready and commissioned emboldened me to eat for lunch any leadership endeavour, especially in my area of interest. This experiences made me a better leader. It built me to lead. So that when I emerged president of my department student union in school. With my team, we were outstanding; pioneering legendary projects that are still visible in the department many years after graduation. For me leadership became a mission, not a position. When you know your 'why', it emboldens you beyond anyone's understanding, so that you are usually seen as weird. In fact, ask anyone who achieves a worthwhile endeavour, the testimony of those around them will always be that they are weird in many ways. You cannot be normal and be extraordinary. But without a deep-rooted 'why', you will not have enough stamina to withstand even those of your household let alone strangers when they come for your head.

You cannot be normal and be extraordinary.

IT IS ABOUT WHAT'S IN YOU

I found that true leaders are distinguished by a unique mental attitude that emanates from an internalized discovery of self, which creates a strong positive, and confident self-concept and self-worth. – Dr Myles Munroe

Leadership starts from what is in you, before what you can give. You can only give accurately when you know what is in you. Every time we miss this perspective, we set out for a life of misery and loneliness in leadership. Unfortunately we have missed it 99% of the times in leadership until now, and hopefully going forward this book will cause a paradigm shift from the erroneous mindset we have held on to for a very long time as we go into this new path - which is the place of knowing yourself first in leadership before reaching out to others. I can almost sense the controversy this new perspective will spark, because it is totally against the norm. And I am excited about it, not for the fun of it, but for the fact that the society has always held on to erroneous conventions until the disruption of an audacious but true idea. It still fascinates me how people and authorities can confidently uphold ideas that keep people in chains and bounds. Man is not meant for the law, the law is meant for man. The law should serve man's purpose, not the other way round.

Your assignment determines your area of leadership.
– Dr Myles Munroe

Leadership puts you in a position to use your potentials. To explore the real you, to savour the beauty of your creation by God, and to maximize the totality of your being. Else you will be leading below your capacity, which limits you from being all that could be. Dr Myles Munroe affirms this when he said in his book, The Spirit of Leadership, that *"your assignment determines your area of leadership"*.

The statement by Plato that "man know thy self" is undoubtedly one of the most profound statements that resonates with the core of human existence. It transcends all the religion and conventions. It is not selfish to find yourself before you give off yourself. In fact giving without knowing yourself can be suicidal. If you do not know that you need a gas mask when suffocating in an aircraft, to keep you alive to be able to save others in similar situation, you will give up your mask. And end up unable to save others and yourself. But the principle that works is that you need to be alive to be able to save others in that situation.

> *It is not selfish to find yourself before you give of yourself. In fact giving without knowing yourself can be suicidal.*

If you do not understand the potency and purpose of the rod in your hand as a leader, you will abuse it. Ask Moses in the Bible, he will probably tell you that after God on the list of his need as a leader, it is the rod in his hand that comes in the order of priority in leading the people to the Promised Land. Without which doom was inevitable.

Ask Moses in the Bible, he will probably tell you that after God on the list of his need as a leader, it is the rod in his hand that comes in the order of priority in leading the people to the Promised Land. Without which doom was inevitable.

When you know your capacity, you maximize leadership.

Leadership puts you in a position to use your potentials, to explore the real you, to savour the beauty of your creation by God and to maximize the totality of your being

---

What you know about 'you' determines your attitude as a leader

They say everything rise and fall on leadership, but leadership rise and fall on attitude, and attitude is a product of self-identity and self-awareness whether negative or positive.

We often hear this phrase, "it is not what you do, but how you do it that makes the difference", the anchor of this statement points to this three syllabic English word 'attitude'. Take away attitude, leadership is dead.

Attitude is the vehicle that delivers leadership substance in any sphere. Attitude is a product of belief affirmed Dr Myles Munroe. Your attitude comes from your belief system, and your belief system is rooted in the knowledge of who you are. What you know about yourself. You can be a particular thing, but if you do not know it, you will likely live in contradiction to that which you are. Which would be unfortunate if it is less than what you really are. A king has an attitude that makes him easily recognizable even in the crowd, simply because of a clear awareness of self.

> *Attitude is the vehicle that delivers leadership substance in any sphere.*

Attitude is key in leadership, and it comes from knowing who you are. And knowing what you possess determines your attitude per time. Your attitude determines 90% of your leadership success. If you have struggled or you are still struggling with identity crisis, you cannot lead successfully. The ideal counsel is to seek help, work on yourself and settle the issue of who you are while you lead, or before stepping into leadership. Especially positional leadership in an organized setting. No time spent on self-discovery is wasted if you must reduce your journey's turbulence to the barest minimum. The principle of garbage in garbage out is true to this finding.

> *No time spent on self-discovery is wasted if you must reduce your journey's turbulence to the barest minimum.*

If you do not know who you are, insecurity is your first nemesis. But knowing who you are breeds confidence; a key ingredient of leadership. This book is however, not focusing on that aspect of leadership. This book is about the very core of leadership that precedes all other aspects of the subject of leadership, which is, why you should lead. It is only commonsensical that you should know why you want to do anything, or engage in any endeavour before you even talk about the skills, abilities, talents, experience or training needed to do it.

If you do not know who you are, insecurity is your first nemesis.

Therefore, after God, leadership is first a self-discovery journey before it is supposed to benefit others. Every marketer understands this principle very well that the knowledge of your product or service will determine the success of sales ultimately. If you do not know your product or service, you will either project it below its capacity or above its capacity. If you do not know your product very well, customers can smell it from afar, and they make a conclusion on action to take regardless of your marketing strategy. So be pleased whenever you are called to lead or situation demands that you lead. Be glad because ultimately you are being called first to appreciate the infinite blessing God the creator has blessed you with. It's a call to the limitless potentials He has bestowed on you, and to appreciate this benevolent gesture from the all-sufficient creator. Secondly you are been called to discover yourself deeper and wider than any other opportunity, or platform can possibly present. And the opportunity to be a better you inevitably becomes a blessing to humanity. This is why you must lead!

Every marketer understands this principle very well that the knowledge of your product or service will determine the success of sales ultimately.

It does not matter who you are or where you are, what you believe about yourself defines your perception about who you are, and everything around you. What you think determines your worth.

Your interpretation of your environment, situations and

people is directly linked to your perception of who you are. Your interpretation determines those you associate with, those you allow into your life, and it determines your destiny because life is essentially about relationships. Dr Myles Munroe in one of his classic thoughts on leadership, relates how the lion sees every other animal in the forest as breakfast, lunch or supper depending on the time of the day, because of the lion's perception of itself. When other animals are seen as a ready meal to the lion, they see the lion as a predator, even those that are more intelligent, stronger or bigger than the lion. The difference is identity based on the knowledge of self. This knowledge of the lion is what gets it excited when in contact with other animals, while other animals shiver when in contact with the lion. The difference in the attitudes is rooted in knowledge of self.

Knowing who you are makes you know what you need or want. You will likely guess wrongly what you want, if you do not know who you are. If you have no clear idea of your content, you will shortchange yourself in your leadership exploit. Your content will determine the kind of experience your container will have. The mentality of a leader's ability determines a leader's success or failure. Thus, a major benefit of your leadership journey is that it helps you to know yourself indeed and in-depth.

Your content will determine the kind of experience your container will have.

Leadership serves you first before it serves humanity.

YOU CANNOT GIVE WHAT YOU DO NOT HAVE

Does this headline above resonate with you? I am pretty sure it does. It is often said that there are three most important relationship in your life. This is what shaped the line of thought of this book, and those three relationships are; relationship with God, relationship with yourself, and relationship with others. The key thing to note here is that your relationship with yourself, or rather your attitude with yourself affects your relationship with everyone else greatly. You cannot be to others what you have not been to yourself first. Neither can you give to others, what you have not yet given to yourself, not because it is intentional, but simply because you cannot give what you do not have.

The capacity in you will find expression when you step into leadership, but note that it is the capacity in you. This is why it is often common to find the personality of a leader permeate, and form the culture of those they lead. It is the capacity in you that is interpreted as experience, and a requirement for certain kind of jobs.

Leadership is inside out, not outside in. When you lead inside out, the world cannot get enough of you. It is simply irresistible! Leading inside out is the most potent, most powerful, most authentic, most genuine, most balanced, most influential and most legendary conduit of leadership. Leading from inside out makes a leader invincible. You will never be more than who you are on the inside. As a man thinks, so is he. Even if external forces made you more than who you really are on the inside, it is only a matter of time before the real you will emerge again. Leading from the inside is simply understanding the three "why(s)" of leadership in this book.

When you lead from inside out, the world cannot get enough of you. It is simply irresistible!

LEADERSHIP HELPS YOU DISCOVER AND MAXIMIZE YOUR POTENTIALS

This forms perhaps the core of what we have been talking about all through this chapter. My greatest times of self-discovery are times when I have had to lead in one capacity or the other. Most times you never fully come to grasp with your abilities, but in the face of a need in leadership.

As much as I am driven to leadership by the ideas that keep popping up in my head, and the passion for innovation that will not give me a break in most instances where I led. My greatest moments of leadership was knowing that my ideas were valid, that I could actually deploy my ideas and thoughts into a product or service that could meet a need. Leadership gives me the opportunity to experiment with my ideas that ultimately forms the vision of my leadership timeline. This illustration played out greatly from being a student leader in the University of Lagos, to leading teams in a couple of projects after school, and of course taken up leadership in various organisations both in career and volunteer service.

Prior to my time as the president of the Students' Historical

Society of Nigeria, I had never been on radio. Maybe I did fantasize about it, but in reality, I had never created a radio content nor anchored any programme on the radio before that time. But the need to innovate in leadership and pass the baton knowing that we had covered new grounds, made me discover my talent in creating radio content, and ultimately present live on radio along with other students with no prior experience whatsoever.

Almost everyone turned down the idea initially, because it has never existed prior to this time, including the school authority who felt radio affair should primarily be the business of the Mass Communication (Masscomm) students. I have learnt that it is normal for your idea to be rejected. It will be unrealistic expectation for you to think everyone will embrace your idea at the first introduction. Reality never works that way.

I have learnt that it is normal for your idea to be rejected. It will be unrealistic expectation for you to think everyone will embrace your idea at the first introduction. Reality never works that way.

However, because we had a deeper conviction of the beauty of our idea, with the right strategy, creativity and passionate communication of this idea, a few of those in authority eventually saw prospect in it. And after the first airing, others who still doubted eventually bought into the vision.

With my executive team, we established a radio programme for the first time in the history of the department called the "Voice of History".

We imagined we could do it, we went to work, and we eventually did it, and discovered we were actually meant to do it. This experience adds to the foundation that forms my chosen career today, which would have been missed if I did not take up the challenge to lead.

> *We imagined we could do it, we went to work, and we eventually did it, and discovered we were actually meant to do it.*

Leadership gave me the opportunity to test my ideas and

prove it to be workable. Today, I basically work and earn a living by birthing ideas, strategizing the success of the ideas and creating words around the idea. Working with ideas form the core of what I do as a career in advertising and communications. Whether it is creating content for marketing communication, or strategizing for business, or creating entertainment content, just name it, every content starts with an idea or combination of ideas, and the ability to cherish ideas and to see it as something as tangible as my physical reality, came from seeing my ideas come to life through serving others on the platform of leadership. And having to test that idea for the sake of meeting a need or solving a particular problem all lend credence to my leadership endeavour.

My friend David Asanga, a leadership expert and inspirational speaker resonate with me as he shares a similar experience with me. Much of his self-discovery journey and leadership engagement is greatly tied to service. His embrace of service at every point made him build leadership capacity. Leadership helped sharpen his talent when he was a class governor in the university, as well as a music director with other campuses in the state under their administration. And now as a professional in his chosen career.

When he was chosen to lead an editorial team during my tenure as president of the department student association, to reawaken a previously comatose academic journal, he stood up to this task with vigor and excellent spirit. This assignment aligned with his talents and passion so that he delivered an excellent work with his team, making the department and school proud of the journal that was published, which they have continued to present as one of the milestones of the department for a long while.

Thus, David had to constantly cultivate his potentials, invest in himself and attract the right company so as to tap from their wealth of wisdom as leaders in various fields and capacity. Stepping into leadership attract great benefits to him and helping him to live a purpose driven life.

He now engages with sharing his leadership experience with people to inspire them, and help them find their purpose in life through seminars, conferences, workshops, trainings, books, radio platforms or any opportunity he gets.

LEADERSHIP PREPARES YOU FOR THE NEXT LEVEL

Leadership prepares you for the next level in any endeavour in life. Responsibility or opportunity to serve always precedes a new level either in career, business, relationship and the likes. Leadership is service, and service is basically solving problem, and anytime you solve problem, you assume a new level of responsibility which is leadership. Responsibility births influence as it put you in position to add value to people's life.

For pastor Grace Ofili, one word that defines leadership is influence; and one-way leaders exert this influence is by serving others. This has always been a recurrent theme in her local church in Lagos, Nigeria. Therefore, long before she became a pastor, she had decided to serve people in a significant way. This led to the birth of Okada Riders Fellowship (ORF) back then, meant to empower the commercial motorbike (popularly known as Okada) riders in her church community and environ.

Having drawn out a plan which encompasses the church objectives, vision, mission, values, services, and strategies, she and her team started a fellowship at a motorcycle park in Ikeja Cantonment, Lagos, Nigeria in late 2001; where they would share God's word, encourage and also pray for members. They were also involved in organizing training and equipping them with safety gadgets like helmets and reflective jackets and so on.

After the bomb blast of 27th January 2002, in Ikeja cantonment, the fellowship spread to other regions in the city, and in a short time it grew from a park to twenty-one parks scattered around Ikeja and environs; and from a few to thousands of riders.

The impact was huge. First, the character of some members, especially those who started coming to church, changed for good. Second, the fellowship members became better at what they were doing in terms of their daily business, as incidences of accidents reduced drastically. Third, they started making more money because they were experiencing change and making the transition from bad to a good lifestyle.

The good news today is, most of them have moved on from commercial Motorcycle business to Tricycle and

Taxi businesses, respectively. Also, while some now have workshops, others have turned from tenants to own their own houses. All this was because Grace and her team took responsibility to lead, serve and influence commercial bike riders around them.

This experience definitely prepared her for what she is doing today as a pastor, but beyond her elevation, the story above shows that her service eventually touched the lives of those around her, and changed their lives forever. While her duty as pastor became effortless as her act of service had prepared her for the position she currently occupies today.

Her story is instructive to serve, to allow God touch lives through you, even while you prune other aspect of your life that might not be ready-made for use, because you cannot truly be successful and consistent in leadership if you do not keep honing your skills and reaching new knowledge frontiers.

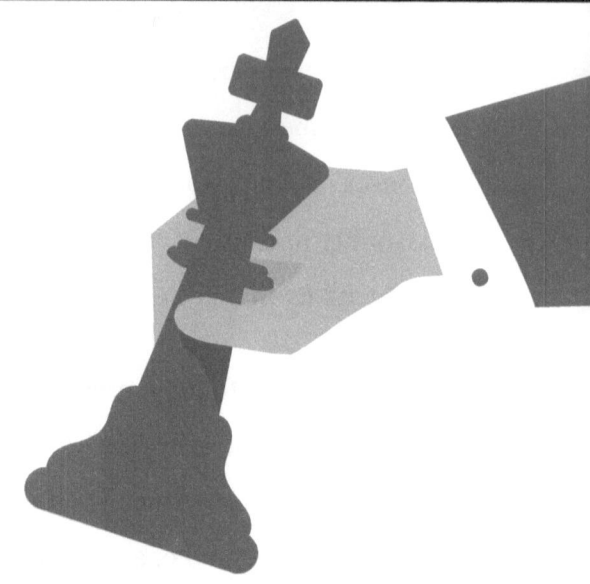

CHAPTER 5

LEAD FOR HUMANITY

O N MARCH 11, 2011, AT 2:46 PM THREE GIANT earthquakes occurred along the edges of tectonic plates approximately 250 miles northeast of the Tohuku or Northeast region of Japan's mainland, otherwise known as Honshu Island. At first, thought to be a single giant earthquake, the series of tremors occurred in succession a mere 6 minutes from start to finish; registering at an unprecedented 9.0 on the Richter scale within the region. The quake resulted in a horizontal sheer displacement of nearly 20 meters on the Pacific floor. So significant was the quake, it was felt across multiple regions ranging from all the way from Chile to Alaska. The resulting tremors unleashed a total of seven waves over a course of 6 hours; the greatest of which hammered the coast with waves as tall as 14-20 meters and reaching as far as 6 miles inland. The catastrophic effects of the 1000-year event far exceeded all design and planning standards – causing destruction to homes, businesses, public services, medical care facilities and infrastructure of all types. The loss of property and services paled in significance to the 28,000 dead or missing across Japan. After early assessments, it was clear that even the complete mobilization of all civil and military forces would be insufficient to support acute and long-term recovery operations. Only with the support of its allies could Japan overcome its greatest obstacle since World War II and bring stability and a renewed sense of hope to its people in the midst of the chaos caused by the largest earthquake in Japanese history.

The facility design standards required that both the primary and backup power supplies (needed to ensure water circulation), were 10-13 meters above ground level. The damage sustained as a result of the tsunami quickly overwhelmed electrical production and distribution systems which in turn raised water temperatures and exposed the radioactive material to the air. The process heat combined with the mixed properties of zirconium, oxygen and hydrogen caused reactors 1 and 3 to explode early the morning of March 12, 2011. The melee of activity over the following 10 days by both Japanese civil and military forces and the international community served as a "game changer" leading to an unprecedented Japanese crisis response and enhanced relations with its most strategic ally, the United States (US).

Almost immediately after the earthquake, United States Forces Japan (USFJ) in conjunction with the United States Pacific Command initiated a 3-Phase Operation "TOMODACHI" to support the Japanese Self Defense Force response and the people of Japan. These operations included involvement from ground, air, and maritime forces working collectively with their Japanese counterparts to provide immediate relief efforts where others could not. [1]

The operation took place from 12 March to 4 May 2011; involved 24,000 U.S. service members, 189 aircraft, 24 naval ships; and cost $90 million. [2]

In the end, Operation TOMODACHI is a bright and glowing example of the ability of US exceptional leadership using its agencies and specifically the Armed Forces, to serve humanity, much more than simply waging war. [3]

You cannot be considered a leading nation or a leader as an individual if all you do is living for yourself. Even if you are given a leadership position, you will lack a key ingredient of leadership which is influence. America (US) understands this principle perhaps more than any other nation in the world, this is why they are the first to show up in crisis situation anywhere in the world. It is what makes a leader and much more what makes them influential. It is at the core of any leadership initiative.

However, whether America's intervention is flawed or not is a different pie entirely. The fact that such interventions have positioned them as a leading nation is the point here. Apart from the case of Japan, America and a few other leading nations of the world have remained key players in providing leadership to most nations of the world through support in times of crisis.

America has remained a leading nation because they walk in this principle of living for others through offering value.

Half of the world's invention is either from America or aided by America. Inventions ranging from technology, engineering, medicine, energy, economy, sport, fashion, just to name a few. This kind of mindset and attitude by a nation has its place in terms of influence in the comity of nations. Simply because they understand that the day you stop giving value, you stop leading. Nigeria assumes the big brother or the giant of Africa due to similar interventions in other African countries, not necessarily because they were the most developed African nation.

The day you stop giving value, you stop leading

This chapter is the last "Why" you must lead, and will likely not be strange to you, as it is the most popular findings of the motive of leadership. Perhaps it is so because it is what brings the ultimate fulfillment as we have been created to live and function within relationships. However, the nature of our relationship with others is the evidence or the fruit of our relationship with God and with ourselves. We will have a sour external relationship if our relationship within is corrupted. A man must first learn about himself and lead himself before he can successfully lead others. An organisation must learn about itself and understand itself before it can be of real value to its target audience. This is why in response to a brief in a business proposal, company or organisations will always attach "about us" page, where they project who they are, and why they are qualified and should be given the client's job. In the same vein in hiring, an organisation will always ask directly or indirectly the question of "let us meet you", to the prospect.

The statement by the Greek Philosopher, "man know thy self" cannot be truer in leadership. In fact, this understanding is needed before any organisation can really identify its target audience. Likewise, the employee in any organisation must understand what the organisation is about, having a good knowledge of its product or service before he or she can sell it effectively. There is nothing as frustrating as being in an organisation you do not really know much about what they do, and you are asked to sell their product or service. I have been there and trust me I do not wish it for anyone. Clarity of purpose with little strategy or idea will win a war compared to great ideas and strategies with blurred understanding or no clarity of purpose. In one of his interviews documented by Catherine Clifford of CNBC, the legendary CEO of General Electric, Jack Welch had something to say about this, *"I have spoken to over a million and a half people over the last 17 years around the world. Suzy [his wife] and I travelled to conference after conference for a while after I retired from the company I was with, we asked that question and we did not get 10 per cent of the crowd knowing where they stood,"* he said. *"If you are a leader and you are a manager, shame on you if people do not know where they stand. You have a moral obligation leading people's lives, talking about their future and not telling them where they stand. It is incredible. It is a shock to me. Every three months, managers should write down for each employee what they are doing well and what they need to improve",* says Welch. [4]

> *Clarity of purpose with little strategy or idea will win a war compared to great ideas and strategies with blurred understanding or no clarity of purpose.*

He went further to say, *"for a large organisation to be effective, it must be simple. For a large organisation to be simple, its people must have self-confidence and intellectual self-assurance. Insecure managers create complexity. Frightened, nervous managers use thick, convoluted planning books and busy slides filled with everything they've known since childhood, real leaders do not need clutter. People must have the self-confidence to be clear, precise, to be sure that every person in their organisation — highest to lowest — understands what the business is trying to achieve. But it is not easy. You cannot believe how hard it is for people to be simple, how much they fear being simple."* Says Welch. [5] This is why the proper progression for leading or serving on any platform or capacity whether as an individual or organisation is for God, for you and for humanity. It is a game of inside out, not the other way round. You become irresistible when you lead from inside out. You lead from inside out when you align with the three whys' which form the immortal truth of leadership.

Having re-echoed and established the above, we cannot overemphasize the urgency attached to your leadership and how it affects the world out there. It does not matter the capacity or the platform from where you are operating from as a leader. Whether you are leading a team of two, hundred or a thousand, whether it is a small family unit or grand royal family fate bequeathed you with, whether you are leading a startup from a garage or a fortune 500 multinational, whether you are leading from a small hamlet that is not even on Google map or from the elevated seats of world powers, your leadership or service will ultimately make meaning when it enriches the lives of others.

You are designed to be a leader or better still to serve because the primary purpose of every one is to impact the world and to be a blessing to it. Your leadership potentials are not meant to end with you. You are a means to an end, not the end. One of the errors observed in most leadership engagement in Africa is that the benefits of leadership enriches the leader only and stops at the leader's table, while true leadership goes beyond the leader and reaches out to the people to benefits them. It is meant for others, it is meant for the world. Chances are you must have heard this time and time again, but it is different and vital when you know that your wellbeing as a leader is dependent on this fact. The level of freshness of a river is directly linked to how much it flows into other channels. A river becomes stagnant and unhealthy when it does not flow into other rivers or connecting body of water. Understanding the three "why(s)" of leadership is what makes a leader balanced and authentic.

As a leader, you are gifted and prepared not to impress or make you bigger than everyone else, your capacity as a leader is to make the world better. This is one of the primary reasons you aspire to leadership, and it is the third and final "Why" in this book. We are quite familiar with this unlike the two previous "Whys" as stated in previous chapters.

Against popular convention, this comes last on the purpose for leadership, because you must be able to appreciate your gift and the Giver, and secondly, you cannot give what you do not have. Your gift, skills, and abilities can serve others because they are of value in itself. You start by serving you first by leading yourself, it is then you can now lead others and let your capability add value to humanity.

It is easy to believe that this is the first motivation for leadership, but history has shown time and time again that you are not considered a true leader if what you offer lacks value, if it does not meet a need, or worse still if it causes pain to people. History is filled with men and women with potentials and capacity who rather than bringing value to the world, instead projected vices and ended up on the dark side of history. The difference between those who fell on the positive side of history and those on the negative side is not that any of them lacked potential or skills for leadership, but because one projected it as value, while the other as vice. The same oratory prowess Adolf Hitler used to compel Germany and its Allies to go into war with the world causing millions of death around the world, and the infamous Holocaust is what Martin Luther King Jr. used to fight for equality during the civil right movement in America. The same audacity and willpower of Idi Amin of Uganda in ruling and enslaving his people is the same used by Lee Kuan Yew to cause Singapore to rise from a third world nation to a first world nation.

Businesses that do not solve a real problem in an innovative way cannot be classified as a leading organisation. Companies like Apple, Nike, Microsoft, General Electric, Amazon, Google, Coca-Cola are considered leading organisations, and they have maintained that status quo over the years because, beyond being a technology, engineering, e-commerce, bevearage or a sport company, they have positioned and established themselves as a company who is out to add value to people, and to make a statement with it. They have realized that helping people to solve a functional challenge is too ephemeral to keep them as No 1 in people's mind, so they elevated themselves to a different status, and that is of value beyond functionality, assuming the position of representing an ideology that resonates with their customers in terms of intrinsic value. These organisations and brands have deliberately, and consistently communicate this fact over the years. If what you are bringing to the table is mere added cost instead of solution, if it has an element of mediocrity, misplaced priority, among other vices, you will be best regarded as everything else but not a true leader.

Businesses that do not solve real problem in an innovative way cannot be classified as a leading organisation.

Living with this consciousness is what makes a person or an organisation indispensable, a consciousness that is fueled by a deep understanding from the CEO to the janitor is what keeps Apple ahead in leading innovation in the tech business the world over. Nobody is confused as to what is happening or what needs to be done, or whose responsibility it is to do it. The understanding of who they are is directly proportional to how much impact Apple has made as one of the world's leading tech behemoth. Simply because they understand that the day they stop offering value to humanity, they stop leading. Influential leadership is not given, it is earned.

Influential leadership is not given, it is earned.

Leading nations or organisation are influential, and influential nations or organisation are leaders. You cannot be considered a leading nation if you are not influential, and you cannot be influential if you are not leading.

Your Fulfillment is on the Ship of Leadership

Looking back to the girl I was from a small town called Spring, I've come a long way. I had dreams of just being a doctor, but now I am also living the dream of impacting lives and making a difference for people. – Dr Nthabiseng Legoete. (GLS 2018)

What will ultimately make life worth the while are not the things you did for yourself, but the life you touched through service. This will most likely sound too cliché to you, and so I wish there is grander or unconventional way to present it to you so that it will not be watered down. If you keep this truth, it will set your life up for ultimate fulfillment. This is the reason why Bill Gates will donate half of his fortune to tackle malaria and Polio in Africa, it is the reason why Warren Buffet will commit all his wealth to humanitarian causes, this is the motive behind great humanitarian and selfless dispositions of people like Michael Jackson, Angelina Jolie, King LeBron James, Mark Zuckerberg, Oprah Winfrey, Nelson Mandela, Mother Theresa, Chief Gani Fawehinmi, Martin Luther

King Jr., Mahatma Gandhi, Zeal Akaraiwai etc.

What will ultimately make life worth the while are not the things you did for yourself, but the life you touched through service.

On the 10th Annual Letter by Bill and Melinda Gates, the couple decided to answer the question of why they give out billions to charity, affirming that what they do provides purpose, this is what they have to say, *"There are two reasons to do something like this,"* the letter says, referring to the $4 billion a year the foundation spends in developing countries trying to end child mortality, distribute vaccinations and improve access to education, plus another $500 million it shares out in the United States. First, *"its meaningful work,"* according to the letter. *"Even before we got married, we talked about how we would eventually spend a lot of time on philanthropy,"* writes Bill. *"We think that's a basic responsibility of anyone with a lot of money. Once you've taken care of yourself and your children, the best use of extra wealth is to give it back to society."* [6]

The emphasis on the response is *"meaningful work"*, simply put they find purpose and fulfillment in doing what they do. Offering to serve using their wealth is what gives them fulfillment ultimately, not necessarily in how much wealth they are able to amass for themselves and family. This is a profound discovery in leadership that the greatest gain is not necessarily in the tangibles like what the bank statement says, but in the intangible like purpose and fulfillment. Your fulfillment is on the ship of leadership, more so purposeful leadership.

The safety of a leader is in offering value to the world.

THERE IS SO MUCH BROKENNESS IN THE WORLD

It is a broken world, you see it in homes, in schools, in offices, in individuals, in organisations, you see in government and state leadership. Most of the anger, reactions and contractions are only a disguised yearning for leadership. You cannot be in the midst of all these and turn away? Or would you?

The world no doubt is in dire need of leadership from the smallest area of influence you occupy, to the neighbours you interact with every day, your leadership is needed. It is believed that whatever pisses you off is a call for you to respond and fix it. Identify one today, study it, build a corresponding capacity and fix it.

It has become inevitable not to step out and lead looking at the level of brokenness in the world today. Brokenness in terms of damages done both naturally and those caused by man. The world is in dire need of leadership. If you do not step out and lead, who is going to save the broken world when disaster or crisis happen, knowing that we are not in essence isolated from any broken part of the world. Even if you are physically far from it, even if you do not have issues you are dealing with in your family, or you are living in a country where leadership is working. If you pay deaf ear to the people who are suffering from failed leadership, it is only a matter of time, the echo of their tragedy will catch up with you. This is why US responds to terrorism in faraway in the Middle East like it is happening on American soil.

The whole of humanity are all connected, an injustice somewhere is an injustice everywhere, and a moral uprightness in one part of the world resonates to the other end of the world. You must lead because we are all connected. The rich in a poor society are more endangered, than the rich in a middle-class society because of this simple reason.

> *The rich in a poor society are more endangered than the rich in a middle-class society because of this simple reason of reverberation effect, and all connectedness of humanity.*

Remember, there is a grand plan somewhere. You have been sent to earth carrying a specific solution to a problem. You are not a mishap on this planet, so do not behave like one. You have been greatly invested in by nature for such a time as this. You are on a mission. You are a super hero. You are an ambassador. Imagine if the famous character James Bond 007, after so much has been invested in training and equipping him for a foreign mission. With millions of dollars spent on the most sophisticated weapon the world will ever produce, all handed over to him to save the world. But, on getting to where he was supposed to carry out that critical assignment that would save the world, he starts behaving like a common citizen of that host country. That will be the biggest blunder that will lead to a catastrophic loss on the entire world. In fact it will be better imagined. In the same vein, it is what plays out anytime you reject leadership or the call to lead.

THERE WILL BE CONTRARY HURDLES

In an interview by Naz Beheshti, a contributor at Women At Forbes who writes about practising mindful leadership and corporate wellness. In Steve Job's honour, she chose to ask a former executive and good friend of Steve's, Mike Slade, what his experience was working for such an iconic leader;

Beheshti: *What is the most helpful criticism you received from Steve?*

Slade: *Steve would help me get out of analysis paralysis. He did not really care about market forces or market share of competitors. He cared about what he could get accomplished.* [7]

This is what great leadership is about, knowing that the

hurdles are high yet sticking to the goal because of the impact the cause will ultimately have on humanity. Great leaders all through history have been fueled by the result of their actions, than being bogged down by the difficulties on the way. The odds against any worthwhile pursuit will always be high, but the impact should be more compelling. If it promises to be easy maybe the gains will not stand the test of time.

Go, gather together all the Jews who are in Susa, and fast for me. Do not eat or drink for three days, night or day. I and my attendants will fast as you do. When this is done, I will go to the King, even though it is against the law. And if I perish, I perish.
– Esther 4:16

To achieve anything worthwhile, there will be hurdles, there will be difficulties. There were hurdles when the Wright Brothers dreamt of flying a heavy metal across the sky, there were hurdles when Martin Luther King Jr., dreamt of equality for all in America, there were hurdles when Nelson Mandela had a vision of a South Africa free from Apartheid, there were hurdles when Henry Ford thought of a vehicle running on engines when all that existed were carts pulled by a horse, there were hurdles when Thomas Edison first thought of the light bulb, there were hurdles when I decided to write this book, hurdles of the mind, environmental hurdles, hurdles of resources tangible and intangible, hurdles of circumstances etc, there are hurdles when Bill and Melinda Gates imagine Africa that is free from Polio and Malaria, there were hurdles when Mary Slessor stood for a time when twins will live in Calabar, Nigeria, there were hurdles when Malala Yousafzai decided to speak up for girls' education in Pakistan. There will continue to be hurdles.

No matter the level of leadership, there will always be hurdles, systemic hurdles, cultural hurdles, spiritual hurdles, people hurdles, knowledge hurdles, tribal hurdles, racial hurdles, gender hurdles, social hurdles, class hurdles, capacity hurdles, 'what will people say hurdles', the list is endless. Leadership is about surmounting the hurdles, there is no great leadership story without layers upon layers of daunting hurdles. But for the understanding of the impact on humanity, leaders have pulled down the walls of difficulties and led humanity into new frontiers with each victory. This is what was explicitly and unequivocally illustrated in the great book that says;

> *Keep your eyes on Jesus, who both began and finished this race we're in. Study how he did it. Because he never lost sight of where he was headed - that exhilarating finish in and with God - he could put up with anything along the way: cross, shame, whatever. And now he's there, in the place of honor, right alongside God.* Hebrews 12:2.

Great leaders understand the concept of this scripture and always arrive at outstanding result every time they follow through.

CONFRONTATION IS NORMAL

Nike Inc., an American multinational corporation which is the world's largest supplier and manufacturer of athletic shoes, apparel and other sports equipment, has attained the status of iconic brand and continue to lead the market solely because they are not afraid of confrontation. They do not play it safe when it comes to a cause they care about, and they go all out for it, not minding stepping on nerves along the way, simply because they understand the 'why' behind their leadership engagement. When you understand that one of the three 'whys' you should lead is to bring progress to humanity in the most genuine way, you will step and confront the impossible.

If you are afraid of confrontation, if you lack the courage to question the status quo, if you faint in an attempt to reach out into a new and most likely unfamiliar horizon in the cause of leadership, you will likely not leave humanity better than you met it. And you will likely have regrets in your later years when you can do close to nothing about it.

Nike has remained legendary because they understand that the impact of the ideology they stand for, is more important than the wellbeing and safety of their brand. Love them or hate them, Nike will continue to lead and determine the conversation for a very long time.

Nike has remained legendary because they understand that the impact of the ideology they stand for, is more important than the wellbeing and safety of their brand.

A 2018 article on Nike's ad campaign featured controversial NFL quarterback Colin Kaepernick, published by Sunny Bonnell for Inc. online platform aptly captured the leadership genius of Nike; According to Sunny Bonnell, *"Nike's action with the Kaepernick campaign Ad was a demonstration of a core principle of leadership that gets ignored, but should not"*. These are the points noted:

They start a needed conversation and getting us to participate in it.

Leaders do not just lead when it is comfortable and everybody's getting along. Anyone can do that. They lead when nobody is getting along and what needs to be said is not being said. That is why I believe that the motivation behind the Kaepernick campaign was not just commercial. I think Nike really cares about racial justice and wants to bring the conversation into the public square whether we are all ready to have it or not.

That is powerful. It positions the company as a moral leader, and a provocative voice that refuses to play it safe when most companies are simply looking to offend as few people as possible. Are you ready to take on that role as a leader? Are you ready to emulate Nike, accept the risk, and possibly change the direction of your brand? Answer these three questions:

Can you achieve your goal without courting controversy?

Your motives here need to be pure. If you can get PR or increase sales by non-controversial means but you seek the headlines anyway, you are just pandering. That is transparent and people hate it.

Do you really believe in the cause?

This is basic. Do not appropriate something like the rights of Native Americans over pipeline companies if it is not in your gut. Everybody will know you are a poseur. On the other hand, if you believe in the cause and have taken the time to educate yourself in it, full speed ahead.

Is what you are advocating likely to alienate at least 50 per cent of the people exposed to it?

That is good; that is you want. It means you are being

provocative and hitting a nerve. You might lose a big chunk of your potential audience but you will gain just as many intensely loyal fans. If the message or cause does not offend, then you are playing it too safe". [8]

"Our lives begin to end the day we become silent about things that matter" – Martin Luther King Jr.

If you are afraid of confrontation, if you lack the courage to question the status quo, if you faint in an attempt to reach out into a new and most likely unfamiliar horizon in the cause of leadership, you will likely not leave humanity better than you met it. And you will likely have regrets in your later years when you can do close to nothing about it. But remember, we are here today in any field of endeavour or any human engagement because somebody tried, somebody reached out, someone asked a question, someone dared to imagine, someone dared to dream, someone dared to confront, someone made the move, someone paid the ultimate price, we are here today because someone decided to lead. They led facing the 'roaring lion' of establishments and systems, they led not afraid of being an outcast and a persona non grata, they led when there was no one to follow, they led not because it was a comfortable experience, but because they knew it was for a worthy cause. They led because they knew humanity cries out for their leadership to push the wheel of progress forward.

IT WILL COST YOU SOMETHING

> *At the end of the day, what have I got? A successful Singapore. What have I given up? My life.*
> *– Lee Kuan Yew*

Leadership will definitely cost you something, whether as an individual, group, business, organisation or nation be ready to pay the price. If anybody tells you it will only be a smooth ride, they are not telling you the complete truth. Leadership is sleeves up, it is getting dirty, it is laying your comfort and life for others, leadership is all the unpleasant things you can think of, it is letting go of your comfort zone. Yet leadership, purposeful leadership is the bedrock of ultimate life fulfillment.

Nigeria and particularly Lagos escaped being turned to a zombie land in 2014 when Ebola hit most Africa countries, owing to the leadership of people who understand that leading is not just a sense of bringing people into comfort and luxury, but more importantly a call to rescue people and generations yet unborn from catastrophe of unimaginable damage. Among the so many known and unknown heroes of Ebola in Nigeria, Dr. Ameyo Stella Adedavoh who paid the ultimate price with her own life to save millions stands out, and then Governor Babatunde Fashola's leadership cannot be overemphasized in this regard.

July 20th, 2014 will remain a significant day in Nigeria when a Liberian Patrick Sawyer flew into Nigeria unknown to the country that he was acutely ill. After collapsing at the airport, Sawyer was wheeled into the emergency unit of the First Consultant Medical Centre (FCMC), a private health facility in Lagos. Under normal circumstances as an ECOWAS official, he should have been taken to a government hospital, but the doctors at all government health facilities were on an indefinite strike so he was taken to FCMC. No one would ever think that he was carrying the deadly Ebola virus in his bloodstream. Here he was in Nigeria, Africa's most populous country Nigeria, and the country's most populous city Lagos made it a double jeopardy.

This was at a time when Liberia, Guinea and Sierra Leone had been declared Ebola epicentres, and all of West Africa was in a panic from being wiped out by this deadly virus. While the rest of the world was praying that Ebola never found its way into Nigeria, a country of over 170 million people. The consequences for the rest of humanity if it did, were better imagined. [9]

Dr Stella Ameyo Adadevoh, the lead physician and Endocrinologist at the First Consultant Clinic, was the one who raised the red flag even though Sawyer was initially diagnosed with malaria. She suspected Sawyer was carrying the Ebola virus. If he was allowed to leave the hospital, the rest of her country would have been in danger. Sawyer was showing symptoms of Ebola from the research Dr Adadevoh had made a while ago on the virus including vomiting, extreme temperature and diarrhoea. She questioned Mr Sawyer about having contact with anyone with Ebola, which he denied. Being the thorough clinician she was, she immediately contacted the Lagos State and Federal Ministries of Health and got him tested for Ebola.

At this point, Sawyer was bent on leaving the hospital on his own terms, but Dr Adadevoh would not have any of it. *"Immediately, he was very aggressive. He was more intent on leaving the hospital than anything else,"* recalls Dr Benjamin Ohiaeri, the Director of First Consultant Hospital, to the BBC. *"He was screaming. He pulled his intravenous tubes and spilt the blood everywhere,"* Ohiaeri added.

Then came the most challenging episode of Dr Adadevoh's leadership in this story, as she stood her grounds and made it clear Sawyer was going nowhere despite the pressure from the patient, and the Liberian government while waiting for the test results. The hospital trusted Dr Adadevoh's judgment. According to Dr Ohiaeri, *"the Liberian Ambassador started calling Dr Adadevoh, putting pressure on her and the institution for denying Sawyer from attending an ECOWAS official retreat. They threatened to sue her because they felt we were kidnapping the gentleman and said it was a denial of his fundamental rights and we could face further actions".* But Adadevoh did not budge, holding him against his will because she did not have a confirmed diagnosis yet, she continued to resist their relentless pressure and said that **"for the greater public good"** she would not release him. She believed it was her call to isolate the index patient, initiate contact tracing technique and inform the health authorities in Nigeria. And she did. [10]

Against all odds, this phenomenon of a woman stood in the gap between a difficult patient whose nation was threatening her with a grave allegation and a nation of millions of citizens at a time when all government health workers were on indefinite strike. According to Dr Ada Igonoh, another physician at the hospital who also contracted the Ebola virus but survived, *"Dr Adadevoh instructed me to write very boldly on his chart that on no account should Patrick Sawyer be allowed out of the hospital premises without the permission of Dr Ohiaeri, our chief medical consultant. All Nurses and Doctors were duly informed".* Igonoh continued: *"During our early-morning ward round with Dr Adadevoh, we concluded that this was not malaria and that* the patient needed to be screened for Ebola Virus Disease (EVD). She immediately started calling laboratories, federal, state ministries and agencies concerned to find out where the test could be carried out".

"Dr Adadevoh at this time was in a pensive mood. Patrick Sawyer was now a suspected case of Ebola, perhaps the first in the country. He was quarantined, and strict barrier nursing was applied with all the precautionary measures we could muster".

"Dr Adadevoh went online, downloaded information on Ebola and printed copies, which were distributed to the Nurses, Doctors and ward maids. Blood and urine samples were sent to LUTH that morning. Protective gear, gloves, shoe covers and face-masks were provided for the staff. A wooden barricade was placed at the entrance of the door to keep visitors and unauthorised personnel away from the patient".

As Igonoh tells it: *"At 6:30 am, Friday, July 25, I got a call from the Nurse that Patrick Sawyer was completely unresponsive. Again I put on the protective gear and headed to his room. I found him slumped in the bathroom. I examined him and observed that there was no respiratory movement. I felt for his pulse; it was absent. We had lost him. It was I who certified Patrick Sawyer dead. I informed Dr. Adadevoh immediately and she instructed that no one was to be allowed to go into his room for any reason at all. Later that day, officials from WHO came and took his body away. We now had the first official case of Ebola virus disease in Nigeria. It was a sobering day."* [11]

Soon after Sawyer passed on, Adadevoh became an Ebola patient herself. Exposure to the index patient had put her life and those of 11 other health workers at First Consultant at risk.

Bankole Cardoso, Adadevoh's only son, told the BBC that his Mum's last moments were jarring. *"From the day the index patient arrived in Nigeria, my father and I were constantly asking my mother and making sure she was OK. We were aware of what could come".*

"I hardly saw her at the time because she was always busy at the hospital, with government officials and the World

Health Organisation officials, and also having to care for this sick patient. She got home at 3am every day, and was up by 7am. I could not see her for about three days and with the Ebola disease, one could not predict the outcome".

"Subsequently, all medical personnel who had contact with him were quarantined based on high risks and low risks. They were isolated and placed under close monitoring and treatment, even though none of their family members were allowed to come close to them". Bankole narrated.

My dad and I went to the centre at Yaba every day, she was fine all along and then suddenly it became apparent. We were seeing little signs and so of course there was panic and confusion. On the first day, I was able to come close and at least stand by the window and have a conversation with her, the second day the same thing, but eventually, we were not even allowed near the window. I did not see her for about 10 days while she was in there.

"I took her things to make her comfortable - towels and slippers and then suddenly the next day I could not even go near the window". He continued. "Then on the Monday we went in and the whole story had changed - they called us into a room and just explained that this is exactly what is going to happen and it is not even a matter of days anymore. It might be hours. That was of course the most crushing time of my life," says Bankole.

"The last time I saw her face-to-face was the day I went to the centre to give her, her footwear and her iPad. She was physically very weak. This was someone I had never seen fall sick in my life. But then, she was physically very weak. I took all the stuff to her and put it through the door, she had to go and collect it because I could not go into the room. We spoke through the window, I was crying. But she was adamant, she said, "Do not worry, son. This thing is not going to kill me, but I am very proud of you." Those were the last words she told me. This was about 10 days before she died. The WHO doctor, Dr. David, told us that it was only a matter of time (before she died), that we should expect the call the next day or in the next week. We were waiting for the call. But he kept telling us that it was a matter of time— it was worse than receiving the actual call. [12]

Dr Igonoh who was also among those quarantined recalls the sober moments before Adadevoh died: *"The following night, Dr Adadevoh was moved to our isolation ward from her private room where she had previously been receiving treatment. She had also tested positive for Ebola and was now in a coma. She was receiving I.V. fluids and oxygen support and was being monitored closely by the WHO doctors."*

"We all hoped and prayed that she would come out of it. It was so difficult seeing her in that state. I could not bear it. She was my consultant, my boss, my teacher and my mentor. She was the imperial lady of First Consultants, full of passion, energy and competence. I imagined she would wake up soon and see that she was surrounded by her First Consultants family but sadly it was not to be."

We have lost a hero.

On August 19, 2014, Dr Stella Ameyo Adadevoh, was certified dead after saving her country by paying the ultimate price. There were 20 Ebola cases in total. 11 were healthcare workers and of those healthcare workers, 6 survived and 5 died, including Dr Adadevoh. [13] She died alongside a pregnant Nurse Justina Ejelonu, and the ward maid, Mrs Ukoh. She was particularly singled out because her heroic act of standing up against the world diplomats and their threats, was the only reason why all 20 Ebola cases in Nigeria were traced to a single path of transmission originating with the first (index) patient. [14]

"We lost some of our best staff. Dr Adadevoh had been working with us for 21 years and was perhaps one of the most brilliant physicians. I worked with her. I know that she was sheer genius," says Dr Ohiaeri. *"By identifying the index patient, it really helped Nigeria to prepare and get ready to trace everybody, and that's the difference between us and our West African neighbours - Guinea, Liberia and Sierra Leone,"* he adds.

Her heroic efforts prevented a major outbreak in the most populous African country and served as the catalyst for successful government action to contain the spread of what would have been a major outbreak in a country of more than 190 million people. [15]

Some events can be forgotten, but certainly not the supreme sacrifice of Dr Adadevoh. She epitomizes how your leadership can benefit humanity so much so that it cost you something. To say she was a very brave woman is an understatement. Her heroic effort saved the nation from the horrific experience because as at that time, doctors in Nigeria were on strike, and that could have caused severe crises that would be nothing but Armageddon not just for Nigeria but Africa and the rest of the world. [16]

> *Some events can be forgotten, but certainly not the supreme sacrifice of Dr Adadevoh.*

The World Health Organisation declared Nigeria Ebola-free on the 20th of October 2014, because of the first act of courage by a woman who stood in the gap for her dear nation risking her own life, at a time when the country was next to nothing in preparation for the deadly virus.

The film "93 Days" is dedicated to Ameyo and tells the story of the treatment of Patrick Sawyer by Adadevoh and other medical staff at First Consultant Medical Center [17]

Prior to the Ebola episode. In 2012, H1N1 (swine flu) spread to Lagos, Nigeria and Dr Adadevoh was the first doctor to diagnose and alert the Ministry of Health. Less than 2 years later, she was again the first doctor to identify another contagious virus – Ebola. It is easy to talk leadership, but the taste of the leadership pudding is in the walking it. What would you do if the fate of a nation is in your hands to decide, at the risk of your own life, just like Dr. Ameyo Stella Adadevoh? Not every leadership engagement will necessarily be a life and death situation, but what is certain is that leadership at any level or platform will definitely cost you something, yet leadership holds the key to your life's fulfillment.

> *It is easy to talk leadership, but the taste of the leadership pudding is in the walking it. What would you do if the fate of a nation is in your hands to decide, at the risk of your own life, just like Dr Ameyo Stella Adadevoh?*

AN OPPORTUNITY TO TOUCH A LIFE

Sometimes in October the year this book was published, a great leader and a senior colleague whose leadership dispositions, her perspective to life and her right judgment inspires me greatly, was involved in a situation most of us would have looked away from. It was an incident that tested the leadership fibres of Lola Olusola. This is a story that reminds us of the daunting and discouraging distance that exist most times between us and touching a life in a positive way. And a story that reveals that leadership is a deliberate endeavour.

On this faithful day, Lola and her hubby were on their way home from visiting some friends late in the evening. She was really tired and reclined the seat to catch some sleep while her hubby drove the car. As they climbed the Gbagada Bridge in Lagos, Nigeria and were midway, her husband drew her attention to a body that he saw on the bridge. She quickly sat up but it was too late to see the body. So she asked him if it looked like a dead body but he said the person looked alive but unconscious.

Immediately, she asked him to let them go back to make a U-turn so they could double check to see if the person was alive before they call the Lagos Emergency number. But then they remembered that he needed to go home as they were expecting some visitors. So they decided he should go home while Lola took the car to check the status of the body.

As she raced on to Anthony area (a neighbouring community to the Gbagada bridge in Lagos, Nigeria) to make a U-turn, she was almost tempted to call the emergency helpline before she confirms whether the person they saw was dead or alive, but due to past experiences, she knew they would ask her if the person was dead, and she could not honestly answer that question since she actually did not see the body. As she climbed on, the body came into view. It sure did not look like she was dead. She looked very much alive but definitely unconscious.

All of these details Lola managed to get within seconds as she could not wait on that bridge. She reasoned that other cars were coming right behind her as the bridge could not take 2 cars side by side. But, deep within her, she knew that her main reason for not waiting was actually because beneath that bridge is the rendezvous point for guys who come to smoke marijuana, where they perpetrate evil and she just could not take the chance of something bad happening to her on that bridge.

As Lola descended the bridge, she called the emergency line. She narrated what she saw. As expected, the person on the phone was quick to ask her if the person was alive. She told him definitely the girl did not look dead to her. So he said they would dispatch an ambulance to the location. He thanked her for the call and ended the call. As she drove home, she felt this sense of unease. So after about 10 minutes, she called them back and asked what the status was. The guy told her that they had got an earlier report before her call and that the previous caller said the girl was dead so they have alerted the relevant agency in charge of picking up dead bodies in the city. By this time, she recalled that the agency's laid back attitude towards saving a life was beginning to get her angry. She told the guy that she made a U-turn just to double check and she looked at the body closely and it sure looked like the person was alive. The guy apologized profusely and said they would dispatch an ambulance immediately.

After series of back and forth with some of the emergency staffs who said unimaginable things, she eventually got through to someone more proficient. She narrated the entire episode and promised them that she was going to put it on social media if nothing was done. The lady sounded professional and apologized on behalf of her colleagues whom Lola had spoken to before.

In the morning of the next day, she called the Lagos emergency line again. After series of display of unprofessional attitude again from the staff of the emergency agency that picked, a lady finally picked who directed her to check the Gbagada general hospital. On getting to Gbagada general hospital, she went straight to the Accident and Emergency section. Fortunately, she met the Doctor who had been on duty the previous night. He said no case like that was brought in by the Lagos Emergency Unit.

She then went to the morgue thinking perhaps the lady had died, yet the body was not there. On her way back, she called her husband to update him, and he advised her to check the bridge again if the body was still there before taking any further action, which she did and to her utter dismay, she saw the body. She drove past the body disappointed and with a heavy heart. She wondered if the girl had a family that longed for her return, praying and hoping that their daughter would return home soon.

After a long battle with the concerned agency, the Lagos state Evacuation team was called to inform them about the 'corpse' on the bridge. And a short while later they came, but discovered that the girl was still alive! However, the van that was brought was for picking corpses and they would have to wait for an ambulance to come and pick the girl. In the meantime, she parked her car, got into their van and they drove to the other side of the road to avoid obstructing traffic, and the risk of being knock down by a vehicle. The next hurdle was waiting for the ambulance. While she called, she encouraged everyone on social media to call the emergency lines to put pressure on them, in order to be prompt with the ambulance needed to save the girl.

After about an hour, the ambulance eventually arrived. She joined the ambulance and when they got to the spot. Alas! The girl was gone! Where did she go? Who carried her? Nothing is adding up. This definitely was the most heartbreaking moment for Lola who had immersed herself in this incident, and took it up even when it was none of her business in a true sense of it. Even when she could have looked away like everyone else. I learnt that leadership might be what we are called for, it takes exceptional leadership to do something worthwhile, and exceptional leadership disposition is usually weird in this part of the world. It is a combination of being deliberate, proactive and ready to pay the price. I mean how can you be so engrossed in a matter you are not at all related to except for the fact we are all humans, and our lives matter? It is very unusual, beyond the call to lead, she understood 'why' she should lead.

After some days, while everything seemed to have gone south and did not make sense anymore to her. And everyone seemed to have moved on, alas! She received the good news. She was informed that the girl was back on the bridge. So around 9.00pm she and her husband decided to drive through the bridge to confirm her location. They saw her sitting on the bridge barricade with her back to the road. Immediately, Lola made necessary calls to get in touch with one of her contacts; a senior officer of the Lagos State Emergency Unit. Judging by her experience in the last 2 days, she felt calling the toll free lines would be an effort in futility.

The Senior Officer sent her team to the place and they were able to pick the girl up early the next morning, and took her to the Gbagada general hospital. A couple of minutes later, Lola joined the ambulance crew at the hospital, from where they moved to Lagos State University Teaching Hospital (LASUTH) and later to the Ministry of Youth and Social Development to get the required documentation that would get her admitted to the Majidun Rehabilitation Center, Lagos, Nigeria.

Few weeks after, when Lola thought that seeing the poor girl, and taking her to rehabilitation centre was the end of the story. She was called to receive an award, the Women Group of the Lagos Chambers of Commerce & Industry during their 4th Annual conference gave her an award in recognition and appreciation of exemplary humanitarian service. This was with respect to the story of the young girl that she had found lying down unconscious on the Gbagada bridge twelve days ago. The award was sponsored by Her Excellency, the Former Deputy Governor of Lagos State; Mrs Sarah Adebisi Sosan.

Furthermore, It will be timely to also note, that this story reveals that sometimes you might not be the one at the epicenter in a leadership engagement, but the seemingly little support you give to those who stick out their neck to lead might be the ultimate game changer for them. Lola hubby's role in this story cannot be overemphasized as his input at every point was highly strategic to the eventual outcome.

Where ever you stand in the course of a worthwhile leadership endeavour, stand like your life depends on it, because it does, as no point is insignificant. You might not be at the centre stage of the performance, but your input from the corner can determine the entire outcome. Even if you have been called to perform the one string instrument in a grand orchestra performance, do not underestimate the impact of your input. Sometimes, it is all that matter. However the sail, remember, you always matter!

Where ever you stand in the course of a worthwhile leadership endeavour, stand like your life depends on it, because it does, as no point is insignificant. You might not be at the centre stage of the performance, but your input can determine the entire outcome.

There is a God waiting for you to express the potentials in you, to serve, to lead, so that you could touch a life for good. Would you say no or yes to that call today?

Everyday life presents us with an opportunity to touch a life, it might not be like the pulsing thrills and grand acts of sacrifice and tenacity like Lola's story. It might just be a seemingly insignificant act of leadership that will mean the world to someone. Do not let it pass, because one good done in one end of the world resonates to the other end of the world. Leadership is what makes the world go round. Remember, you cannot give out value without getting back value.

The Strategies are Infinite

There are books and materials on how to overcome your hurdles in leadership whether as an individual, group or organisation, but every military operation knows that at the first strike every strategy ends and you start to follow your intuition and your guts. You lean on a higher force that is connected to your inside.

You have known enough. It is time to do, it is time to

become. No more standing arms akimbo, it is time to roll your sleeves up and work. It is time to roll your sleeves up and serve. It is time to roll your sleeves up and lead.

Tomorrow is not guaranteed, today and now is all you have, and all that is 100% sure. Make the most of the most of it.

The universe does not support vacuum, something is meant to fill every space. Something is naturally designed to occupy vacuum. The same way something or someone must always lead. Whether you like it or not. If good is not deliberate, evil will prevail. If excellence is not deliberate, mediocrity will prevail. If standard is not deliberate, substandard will prevail. If mindfulness is not deliberate, mindlessness will prevail. If leadership is not deliberate, clueless followership that lack vision, and purpose will prevail. The call to leadership is not optional, it is not secondary. The call to leadership is mandatory and primary to existence.

If good is not deliberate, evil will prevail. If excellence is not deliberate, mediocrity will prevail. If standard is not deliberate, substandard willprevail. If mindfulness is not deliberate, mindlessnesswill prevail. If leadership is not deliberate, clueless followership that lack vision, and purpose will prevail.

Identify areas, platforms or situation where your talent, skill or experience is needed, and serve. Be sensitive to moments that will demand for your leadership capacity and own it. Serve with your heart, soul and mind. Pour into it an endearing legacy, because you have been born to do it, so just do it. For God, for you and for humanity.

Lead!

REFERENCES

Chapter 2

1. African Success. (2015). Biography of Dora NKEM AKUNYILI, www.africansuccess.org http://africansuccess.org/visuFiche.php?id=463&lang=en

2. Muo, Ik. (2014) Pharm. Dora Akunyili, Leadership, Achievement And Performance. Business Day, https://swankpharm.wordpress.com https://swankpharm.wordpress.com/2014/07/22/pharm-dora-akunyili-leadership-achievement-and-performance/

3. African Success. (2015). Biography of Dora NKEM AKUNYILI, www.africansuccess.org http://africansuccess.org/visuFiche.php?id=463&lang=en

4. IBRAHIM, AKINWUMI. (2017). Remembering Dora Akunyili, one of Nigeria's brightest stars, https://www.thecable.ng https://www.thecable.ng/remembering-dora-akunyili

5. Muo, Ik. (2014) Pharm. Dora Akunyili, Leadership, Achievement And Performance. Business Day, https://swankpharm.wordpress.com https://swankpharm.wordpress.com/2014/07/22/pharm-dora-akunyili-leadership-achievement-and-performance/

6. IBRAHIM, AKINWUMI. (2017). Remembering Dora Akunyili, one of Nigeria's brightest stars, https://www.thecable.ng https://www.thecable.ng/remembering-dora-akunyili

7. African Success. (2015). Biography of Dora NKEM AKUNYILI, www.africansuccess.org http://africansuccess.org/visuFiche.php?id=463&lang=en

8. IBRAHIM, AKINWUMI. (2017). Remembering Dora Akunyili, one of Nigeria's brightest stars, https://www.thecable.ng https://www.thecable.ng/remembering-dora-akunyili

9. Willow Creek Association. (2018). http://www.willowcreek.com http://www.willowcreek.com/events/leadership/#faculty

10. Qualihealth. (2018). http://www.qualihealth.co.za/ http://www.qualihealth.co.za/about

11. Willow Creek Association. (2018). Quality and Affordable Healthcare—Nthabiseng Legoete—GLS 2018 Faculty Spotlight, https://globalleadership.org https://globalleadership.org/news-and-updates/one-doctors-vision-provides-quality-healthcare-to-thousands-2018-faculty-spotlight-nthabiseng-legoete/

12. Willow Creek Association. (2018). Quality and Affordable Healthcare—Nthabiseng Legoete—GLS 2018 Faculty Spotlight, https://globalleadership.org https://globalleadership.org/news-and-updates/one-doctors-vision-provides-quality-healthcare-to-thousands-2018-faculty-spotlight-nthabiseng-legoete/

13. Willow Creek Association. (2018). Quality and Affordable Healthcare—Nthabiseng Legoete—GLS 2018 Faculty Spotlight, https://globalleadership.org https://globalleadership.org/news-and-updates/one-doctors-

vision-provides-quality-healthcare-to-thousands-2018-faculty-spotlight-nthabiseng-legoete/

14. McClain, Trey. (2018). GLS 2018: Session 7 – Dr. Nthabiseng Legoete, http://treymcclain.com http://treymcclain.com/gls-2018-legoete/

15. McClain, Trey. (2018). GLS 2018: Session 7 – Dr. Nthabiseng Legoete, http://treymcclain.com http://treymcclain.com/gls-2018-legoete/

Chapter 5

1. Wilson, Rockie K. (2012). Operation TOMODACHI: A Model for American Disaster Response Efforts and the Collective use of Military Forces Abroad, https://www.omicsonline.org https://www.omicsonline.org/open-access/operation-tomodachi-a-model-for-american-disaster-response-efforts-and-the-collective-use-of-military-forces-abroad-2167-0374.1000108.php?aid=7466

2. Wikipedia, (2018). Operation Tomodachi, https://en.wikipedia.org https://en.wikipedia.org/wiki/Operation_Tomodachi

3. Wilson, Rockie K. (2012). Operation TOMODACHI: A Model for American Disaster Response Efforts and the Collective use of Military Forces Abroad, https://www.omicsonline.org https://www.omicsonline.org/open-access/operation-tomodachi-a-model-for-american-disaster-response-efforts-and-the-collective-use-of-military-forces-abroad-2167-0374.1000108.php?aid=7466

4. Clifford, Catherine. (2017). Jack Welch: This is the No. 1 key to success as a leader, https://www.cnbc.com https://www.cnbc.com/2017/11/17/former-ge-ceo-jack-welch-how-to-be-a-great-leader.html

5. Clifford, Catherine. (2017). Jack Welch: This is the No. 1 key to success as a leader, https://www.cnbc.com https://www.cnbc.com/2017/11/17/former-ge-ceo-jack-welch-how-to-be-a-great-leader.html

6. Clifford, Catherine. (2018). Bill and Melinda Gates: This is why we give our billions away, https://www.cnbc.com https://www.cnbc.com/2018/02/13/why-bill-and-melinda-gates-give-away-billions.html

7. Beheshti, Naz. (2018). Remembering Steve Jobs: A Visionary Leader Who Changed The World, https://www.forbes.com https://www.forbes.com/sites/nazbeheshti/2018/10/05/remembering-steve-jobs-a-visionary-leader-who-changed-the-world/#7af3e604ced7

8. Bonnell, Sunny. (2018). Love Them or Boycott Them, Nike's Leading in One Critical Way. What Is It?, https://www.inc.com https://www.inc.com/sunny-bonnell/nike-has-shown-one-quality-that-all-great-leaders-have-what-is-it.html

9. Egbas, Jude. (2017). 3 years ago, this hero saved Nigeria from the deadly Ebola, https://www.pulse.ng https://www.pulse.ng/news/local/3-years-ago-dr-stella-adadevoh-saved-nigeria-from-ebola-id7173942.html

10. Dr. Ameyo Stella Adadevoh Health Trust. (2018). DR.

AMEYO STELLA ADADEVOH, https://www.drasatrust.org/ https://www.drasatrust.org/dr-adadevoh

11. Oyibode, Austin. (2017). The life and times of Dr. Stella Ameyo Adadevoh who paid with her life to save Nigeria from Ebola virus, https://www.legit.ng https://www.legit.ng/1112099-the-life-times-dr-stella-ameyo-adadevoh-paid-life-save-nigeria-ebola-virus.html

12. Deolu. (2015). MY MUM'S LAST DAYS – DR STELLA ADADEVOH'S SON OPENS UP, http://www.informationng.com http://www.informationng.com/2015/05/my-mums-last-days-dr-stella-adadevohs-son-opens-up.html

13. Dr. Ameyo Stella Adadevoh Health Trust. (2018). DR. AMEYO STELLA ADADEVOH, https://www.drasatrust.org/ https://www.drasatrust.org/dr-adadevoh

14. Oyibode, Austin. (2017). The life and times of Dr. Stella Ameyo Adadevoh who paid with her life to save Nigeria from Ebola virus, https://www.legit.ng https://www.legit.ng/1112099-the-life-times-dr-stella-ameyo-adadevoh-paid-life-save-nigeria-ebola-virus.html

15. Dr. Ameyo Stella Adadevoh Health Trust. (2018). DR. AMEYO STELLA ADADEVOH, https://www.drasatrust.org/ https://www.drasatrust.org/dr-adadevoh

16. Wikipedia. (2018). Ameyo Adadevoh, https://en.wikipedia.org https://en.wikipedia.org/wiki/Ameyo_Adadevoh

17. Wikipedia. (2018). Ameyo Adadevoh, https://en.wikipedia.org https://en.wikipedia.org/wiki/Ameyo_Adadevoh

ABOUT THE BOOK

The subject of leadership has always been on the top burner in any sphere, from individuals to groups, to organisations, to brands, to businesses and nations.

Everything has always and will continue to revolve around leadership. This has led to the sprung up of materials on how to be a better leader, or how to simply lead in any given moment or platform.

And true to this, there has been inexhaustible materials on this subject of leadership so that it has become an over-saturated topic, where everyone has an idea what leadership is or should be. Which is good when knowledge shakes hands with action.

But! No one has actually asked the most vital question in all these discussions, and that is;

Why Must You Lead?

Why Should You Choose To Lead?

Why Should You Be The Leader?

Why Should You Lead?

Why You?

Why Not Another?

All through the ages, the question of How, Where, Whom, What, When and Where has been repeatedly attended to when it comes to Leadership. But the most important question of WHY has been left unattended to. Even those that tried to proffer answer could not do justice to it, because they had little or no idea.

And because we have not asked this vital question, humanity has suffered brutally due to this knowledge gap in leadership.

Yes, you can know the "how" to do something. You can know the "what" in doing something or being something. And you can know the "where or when" in doing something or being something, but if you cannot answer the big question of "WHY" you should be something or doing something, you will be brought to your knees at the slightest opposition.

If you do not know "why" you do what you do, or if your "why" is not strong enough, you will be knocked out of the ring of life every single day.

This book succinctly answers that most important question of leadership that no one has ever asked before now. The ultimate question of WHY! A fresh perspective that holds the key to becoming an extraordinary leader whether as an individual, brand or organisation.

In this book, you will learn all that is needed for you to lead with "Why".

Why You Must Lead.

MEET THE AUTHOR

Ernest Ademola Ehigie is a passionate and purpose-driven young man on a mission to bring about God's agenda in Leadership/Governance, Media, Tech and Ministry to shape culture and influence lives for greatness.

He is a thought leader and advocates for excellence in any leadership endeavour. A vision-driven nation builder, innovator, social influencer, who is passionate about the establishment of democratic, strong government institutions and systems that meet people's need.

A multi-talented, skilled and experienced Marketing and Communications Expert with global and local brands in his portfolio. An exceptional Copywriter, Content Developer, Creative Writer, Poet, Adman, Nation Builder, Conference Speaker, and Tech Enthusiast. He is the founder of 5 Syllables.

He also serves in various not-for-profit organisations that focus on causes like leadership, good governance, business, entrepreneurship, health, faith, and socio-economy.

Copyright © 2018 Ernest Ademola Ehigie
Amazon: Amazon.com/author/contentking
LinkedIn: https://www.linkedin.com/in/ehigieernest/
Twitter: @IAmContentKing
Instagram: @iamcontentking

Email: officialcontentking@gmail.com

Created by
5 Syllables

www.ingramcontent.com/pod-product-compliance
Lightning Source LLC
Chambersburg PA
BHW021409210526
463CB00001B/293